ALASKAN DEEP SEA FISH TALES

ALASKAN DEEP SEA FISH TALES

A SELECTED GROUP OF SHORT STORIES
ABOUT GUIDED CHARTER BOAT
OPERATIONS IN ALASKA

TRUE STORIES ABOUT ACTUAL INCIDENTS
THAT HAVE OCCURRED ABOARD
THE AUTHOR'S CHARTER BOAT
BIG FISH, BIG STORMS, AND BIG BREAKDOWNS

FUNNY, SERIOUS, AND SOMETIMES DUMB

WRITTEN BY THE OWNER OF
FANTASY NORTH CHARTERS

KENNETH A. COPE

ALASKAN DEEP SEA FISH TALES

Copyright, 1999 by Kenneth A. Cope

No part of this book may be reproduced in any form or by any means without express permission in writing by the publisher or author. Permission and/or information can be obtained through Fantasy North, P.O. Box 211, Seldovia, Alaska 99663.

All Rights Reserved. Printed in the United States.

Published by Fantasy North

Library of Congress Catalog Card Number: 99-94691

ISBN 0-9670108-0-2

Ben Cope
'2004

ALASKAN DEEP SEA FISH TALES

This Book Is Dedicated to
My Wife and Daughter
Who Believed
It Could Be Done

ALASKAN DEEP SEA FISH TALES

TABLE OF CONTENTS

Introduction -1
The Big Oops -3
Seasickness Can Be costly - 7
Man vs. Woman/King Salmon Fishing - - - - - - - - - - - - 11
The Old Man & The Wish - 17
An Interesting Fourth of July - - - - - - - - - - - - - - - - - - 23
Dad, Oh My Gawd - 29
High Expectations -35
The Encounter - 41
Female Philosophy - 47
Fly Fishing For Halibut-Almost - - - - - - - - - - - - - - - - -53
The Summer From Hell - 57
Fish & Game - 65
The Unexpected Can Happen - - - - - - - - - - - - - - - - - 71
The Japanese/Waste Not - 77
Midwestern Size Adjustment - - - - - - - - - - - - - - - - - - 83
Our Problem=Their Rescue - - - - - - - - - - - - - - - - - - -89
The Tow - 95
The Voyage - 101
An Airplane Story -109

ALASKAN DEEP SEA FISH TALES

INTRODUCTION

The book you are holding contains a number of short stories about unusual and especially memorable days experienced aboard the authors charter boat while operating on Lower Cook Inlet and Kachemak Bay, Alaska. This area of ocean is approximately one hundred and forty air miles South of Anchorage.

All of the incidents written about in this book are true. Names and dates have been deliberately left out in most situations but each and every one of these stories happened in real life.

This book represents the authors first attempt to tell about the trials and pleasures of running a small tourist oriented seasonal business in Alaska. It is a sincere attempt to convey the variety of conditions, circumstances, and personalities that interact daily in the hectic, seasonal fishing charter industry.

The privilege I feel, to have had these experiences and to have shared them with clients is quite difficult to express. I have done and seen and experienced things as a charter captain, that few people in the entire world have been

ALASKAN DEEP SEA FISH TALES

lucky enough to partake of. I hope anyone reading these stories will enjoy reading them and vicariously get a small taste of what Alaska fishing is like and feel the joy, the fear, the frustration, and the shared successes.

ALASKAN DEEP SEA FISH TALES

THE BIG OOPS!

Soon after I began operating as a charter boat skipper, I was still learning the ropes, so to speak, about customer relations. In other words, I was learning to handle all types of worries and concerns from sometimes inexperienced, sometimes fearful, always excited, clients.

As the clients boarded the boat at the dock each morning, I was becoming accustomed to the never ending barrage of questions about boat, gear, water and fish. Each skipper develops his or her own individual pattern of answers, and being a relatively new fishing guide, I was especially proud to be assuring people their day would be a fun experience, that they would in all likelihood catch fish, and they would all be comfortable with each other and the equipment before the day was over.

One morning I was happily greeting my diverse group of fishermen and women, as they made their uncertain way aboard my thirty foot Bayliner, tied to the mooring in Seldovia. While these potential fish catchers made their way aboard, my attention was drawn to a rather seriously rotund, middle aged woman who was very nervous about falling in the water. She was afraid the dock would shift

ALASKAN DEEP SEA FISH TALES

and dump her in the ocean as she approached the boat. After boarding she was concerned about the boat overturning or sinking. I reassured her over and over again that there was nothing to fear and she would have a great time. Finally, we were ready to leave the harbor and hit the fishing grounds.

The morning was a comparatively calm one by Alaskan standards. Three foot seas with a ten to fifteen knot southerly wind. Not flat, but extremely fishable.

We made the trip to the selected fishing spot of the day and were soon setting lines on the bottom, waiting for the Halibut to start striking. The rocking motion of the boat was perfect to entice good solid strikes, but not enough to cause much concern about seasickness or falling accidents. In a short time nearly everyone was hooking up and landing fish, getting more excited with each new strike on the baits.

The rather large lady was not hooking up. She steadfastly but good-naturedly refused to go anywhere near the railing of the boat and was attempting to fish with only the very tip of the rod over the side of the boat. Hanging on to the large, heavy, deep sea rod and reel with only one hand, using the other to secure a handhold on anything she could. Staying as close to the cabin door as possible.

I started paying close attention to her rod, wanting to help her catch at least one fish, and hopefully get her past her

ALASKAN DEEP SEA FISH TALES

fears of falling overboard. I also didn't want to break a rod tip off if she did hook up. Shortly I saw indications of a good sized fish mouthing her bait, and told her to get ready. Steadying the rod body for her, while lending my other arm for support I managed to get her half-way to the boat rail when the fish struck solidly. Immediately the rod was pulled down forcefully in an arc that signaled, very big fish.

Numerous things happened in the next few seconds. She immediately grabbed the rod in both hands and started shouting. "Its going to pull me in the water." Repeating this phrase several times, she was taking baby steps towards the side of the rocking boat at the same time. Nearing the edge of the boat rail with the main section of the rod, I was intending to help her set the thick base of the rod on the rail, this would enable her to wind the crank on the reel with one hand and steady the rod base with the other, allowing most of the strain to be balanced on the railing.

By now she was screaming at the top of her voice that the fish was going to pull her into the water, I was equally loudly screaming that it would be okay, just let the fish finish running until it was tired, then we would start the long process of reeling in the big Halibut. During the seconds that this was all happening, the reel continued to shriek out the song of a large fish running, stopping only for milliseconds and going again. Reaching the rail, I was satisfied we were going to get things under some kind of control momentarily. Turning to her as I laid the thick padded base against the chrome railing, I was startled to see her eyes literally bulging out of her head in fear. I was reaching out to grab the rod when the fish made another hard move pulling forcefully on the line. At this time she just let go of everything. The strain on the line snapped the rod over the side and into the dark rolling water in less than a heartbeat.

There was sudden silence on the deck as I incredulously asked what on earth had possessed her to let go of the pole. Her answer was an embarrassed, Oops, I guess I shouldn't have done that. The other clients, waiting for the expected explosion from me, from the loss of an expensive rod and reel, nervously started to snort and chuckle at her and my discomfort.

There were a few seconds when I wasn't sure if I was going to get mad or disgusted. The loss of the gear was bad, but the fish on the other end of the gear is what really mattered. One of the other fishermen aboard then started to parody what had happened with his own rod, mimicking the tiny steps toward the side of the boat. In an instant the comedy of the situation took over and we were all laughing so hard tears were running down our faces in the cold wind. The rest of the day was a great success, and the lady that lost the rod graciously paid for its replacement.

ALASKAN DEEP SEA FISH TALES

SEASICKNESS CAN BE COSTLY

This particular morning the schedule called for there to be four fishermen aboard. All men, three of them were young Alaskan construction worker types. These three were what I call regulars. Fishermen or groups that have fished with me more than once in the past. With the regulars, you always have a better feel for what the day is going to be like, as far as fishing personalities. I knew these guys to be fun people and aggressive Halibut fishermen. The fourth party, I did not know.

Everyone arrived on time, as they usually do, and after the normal round of introductions, safety briefing, and other boat type conversations, we left the harbor and headed out to the grounds. During the conversations my fourth person had identified himself and stated he worked as a lawyer for one of the larger Anchorage firms. He was young appearing also and was as anxious as anyone to hit the fish. The ride out was constant conversation and swapping of fishing stories. I concluded we would have a smooth day of it as all parties seemed to hit it off and the beginnings of a good fishing team seemed to be forming up. Congeniality is vitally important on a six pack boat, for a really good day.

ALASKAN DEEP SEA FISH TALES

Running the boat out this day was an easy drive, with smooth four foot swells, spaced fairly closely, no wind at all to speak of, and a light fog rising off the slick water. The promise of a good Kachemak Bay fishing day was ahead.

Reaching the desired area, I stopped the boat and started rigging lines for fishing. The three regulars pitched in, knowing the drill from previous trips, and we were ready to fish in short order. Soon we had four lines down and fish hitting steadily. A skippers dream.

After only a few minutes of fishing time, my fourth, the lawyer from Anchorage, said he wasn't feeling well and was going to sit down in the cabin for awhile. This isn't too abnormal, seasickness happens to about one out of four people. I assured him that the feeling would probably pass soon and to try to just relax. Thinking to reassure him more I added the comment. "The water is great today. If you can put up with it for five or six hours, we'll be back at the dock." His look back at me didn't say he was at all reassured.

His sick feeling didn't pass. In a very short time he was violently seasick. Usually once a person heaves, they get some better. This person only got worse, a lot worse, and very quickly too.

ALASKAN DEEP SEA FISH TALES

The other three fisherman were having a great time and giving the sick one the normal macho hoo ha. Picking on the sick person always seems to be fun, for the not sick ones. They were landing fish regularly and it looked as if we would have an easy, limit out day. It was not to be.

After about thirty minutes of steady retching into a bucket, over the side of the boat, and all over the deck of the boat, my lawyer client miserably said. "Skipper we have to go in, I can't take this any more." This brought loud negative comments from the rest of the crew, and more assurances that he would get better soon. The next fifteen minutes was more of the same, only worse. Soon he was virtually laying on the wet messy deck, rolling back and forth with the wave movements, getting wet and sicker all the time. I tried to get him into the cabin and into a seat, but he wouldn't have any part of going inside, where he would have to smell himself. By now the smell was getting rather distinct. After the worst yet, bout of retching, he pulled himself up against the side of the fishing deck and said. "Skipper we're going back to town, now." Again cries of dismay from the other fishermen. Ignoring them, smeared from head to foot with nasty looking unidentifiable stuff, and soaking wet, he said. Using as decisive tones as he could manage. "Skipper we're going to town right now. If I have to buy the Damn boat, we're going to town, now!" More howls of indignation and negative responses, from the others.

ALASKAN DEEP SEA FISH TALES

I tried one last time to get him to go into the cabin and try to stick it out. He wasn't having any part of it, all he wanted was to get back on dry land. Turning to the other clients aboard he told them, while still retching and gagging. "Guys, I'm really sorry about this, but we are going in. I was completely serious about buying the boat, if necessary. I feel like I'd have to get better to die. I'll pay for all of your expenses for the day. Everything you spent money on getting here, I'll write you a check and pay the skipper for the trip. But, we are going in, now."

The three regulars looked at each other and then at me, for some sign this was a joke. I assured them that he was totally serious and I guess the fishing was over for this trip. Shaking their heads in disbelief, they started winding up the baits and preparing for the trip back to the dock.

When we arrived back in the harbor, it was only a few minutes before the lawyer was feeling much better. Such is the action and reaction to seasickness. After taking more ribbing than he really deserved, he wrote out a check for everybody, then reimbursed the others for their incidental costs. After finishing the payoffs, he turned to me and laughingly said. "Best damn money I've spent in I don't know how long."

# ALASKAN DEEP SEA FISH TALES

MAN vs. WOMAN-KING SALMON FISHING

Back in the earlier days of my charter fishing experiences, in the early 1980's. I had accepted a charter, from a young couple, to troll for King Salmon up off of Anchor Point and Deep Creek. Since the day was forecast as perfect and there were only two people chartered, I invited my wife to come along for the day. Salmon trolling is not the most activity intensive fishing there is, and I thought it would be a nice way to spend the day, and still get some payment for it. The day was beautiful, warm, clear, and the water on the ocean was absolutely glass flat.

Before getting too deep in this story, I should explain that I have never been extremely lucky or skillful in catching King Salmon. Particularly back in those days. For numerous years I had tried and tried to learn the magic trick to make them hit. I fished with some exceptional King Salmon fishermen and watched lots of fish landed, but they just didn't seem to like what I did to the lure, bait, pole, or whatever. Halibut, I can murder them, and even the other species of Salmon. King Salmon however, remain a challenge to me each year.

ALASKAN DEEP SEA FISH TALES

We left Seldovia about seven in the morning, had an uneventful run over thirty miles of flat calm ocean. Saw many otters, seals, and even a pod of porpoise, all adding to the excited feelings everyone was experiencing. We reached the waters off of the Anchor River about two hours from the tide turn. I was feeling very optimistic, with the water and weather so fine, who wouldn't be. The scenery to the West, of the Alaska Range was stupendous to say the least and the atmosphere on the boat was more of a day trip picnic, than a charter. There were numerous other boats in the area, some fishing for Halibut, but most rigged for trolling Kings.

Setting two rods up on the stern for trolling, attaching the downriggers, baiting, etc. took only a few minutes and we were ready to nail fish. After talking it over with my wife, it was decided that the girls would run the boat and the guys would watch the rods. It's not often that the skipper on a charter gets to actually fish, so I thought this was great, and I was looking to break out of my King Salmon curse. After getting the boat lined out and instructing my wife on what to watch for on the sonar, I anxiously exited the cabin to watch those rod tips.

The boat was slowly moving up the coast, the scenery and weather pristine perfect, companionship was great, and the rod tips were working steadily, with great twitching and popping as the big flashers and cut bait worked below.

ALASKAN DEEP SEA FISH TALES

Within ten or fifteen minutes both rods had soft hits but no hookups, after another few minutes I decided to check the condition of the bait, and told the other man fishing, to check his at the same time. Just as we reached for the rods there were simultaneous hits on both. Yelling for my wife to put the engines in neutral, I grabbed a rod and started working the fish, as did the other fisherman. There was lots of hollering and excitement as the drags on the medium weight gear were worked by the fish. Boy, less than thirty minutes into the day and we had two fish hooked up, life can be good!

After some acrobatics switching rods around due to the fish swimming in circles, we finally got down to the serious business of landing these two salmon. My client made more headway with his fish, and as it was starting to get close to the boat, I had his wife take the pole I was using, while I intended to net his fish. She was capable with the rod and knew at least the basics of working a fish, so I concentrated on the fish nearing the surface. Looking into the murky water I saw color, but not the silver color of an ocean run salmon. He had hooked one of the largest Gray Cod I had ever seen. It was at least twenty-five pounds. Not what we were looking for!

Seeing what he had, made me lose interest in that rod, we still had a good one on the other rod. I quickly moved to the other side of the boat, while telling him to not worry about boating the big Cod, just let it lay in the water till we boated his wife's fish. Her fish was a dandy I was sure. It

ALASKAN DEEP SEA FISH TALES

wanted to stay deep and had the feel of a really big King. After what seemed to be an eternity, the fish was nearing the boat. Looking down in the water again, sure of a big salmon this time, I was dumbfounded to see a sixty pound Halibut looking back at me instead of the salmon I wanted so badly. We landed the Halibut, which excited the clients a lot, turned the Cod loose, and re-rigged for the Kings again.

The next eight hours went by without as much as a nibble on the baits. We tried every trick I knew, but nothing was working. Shallow water, deep water, different bait set ups, lures. About five o'clock, my wife started to complain of being tired of sitting behind the wheel of the boat and made several suggestions that amounted to, lets go home we aren't going to catch them today. After another hour of this I was just about ready to agree and took over the wheel of the boat.

Turning the boat South and close inshore I started one last run down the coast. My wife and the wife of the other fisherman took their places manning the working rods. We hadn't gone fifty yards when a massive hit took my wife's bait. The reel screamed in protest over and over as the fish fought to shake the hook. Frantically we reeled in the other gear and started working the fish. As the other rod was stowed, my wife's fish jumped completely out of the water, shaking its head, sixty or seventy yards behind the boat. A King and a nice one too! Now everyone was really excited and pandemonium ruled the boat as she fought the fish and

ALASKAN DEEP SEA FISH TALES

we worried about losing it. Finally the big fish was worn out and beside the boat. We netted it without incident, and were all jubilant, we had a King, lets go home. It turned out to weigh fifty-three pounds.

My wife was suddenly not tired or bored or ready to go home. She insisted that the girls get another chance to catch one more King. Arguing with her that it was getting late, and we had fished all day with only one fish, did no good.

Without much hope I agreed to do one more run of no more than thirty minutes, then we would have to start in. Everybody agreed and the lines were soon ready to deploy again. My wife insisted we set the lines out very close to the beach. She was convinced the westerly sunlight shining on the shallow water would attract fish in close. I disagreed but ran the boat in as close as I felt comfortable with, about twelve feet of water under the boat.

The lines were set out and we started trolling South once again. You already know what happened. We hadn't hardly moved when both lines were hooked up on Kings. Things got very interesting for a few minutes as I tried to not lose either fish and move the boat off of the beach a little further. After a proper amount of time had passed, we managed to boat both fish, one was thirty-eight pounds and the other was forty-two.

ALASKAN DEEP SEA FISH TALES

We had a beautiful ride back to Seldovia. Both of the women were in heaven, and they couldn't stop ribbing us guys, all the way home. We took it good naturedly, but it sure put our male egos away for a while.

ALASKAN DEEP SEA FISH TALES

THE OLD MAN & THE WISH

One of my long time customers called, wanting to book a trip for himself, his elderly father, and three of his work related friends. This was a spur of the moment trip but, by coincidence, I did have an available opening in the time frame they needed.

After talking for some time about upcoming tides and expected weather, we had set all of the arrangements in place. Just before hanging up he told me his father was in poor health. He and his father had talked, over the years, about fishing for Halibut. But for all the usual and various reasons, they had never managed to do the Halibut trip. Now his father was failing and they had decided this might be the last opportunity for them to do it, before age and deteriorating health, prevented it from happening.

The morning of the trip was one of perfect weather, visibility was probably two hundred miles or more. The sky was cloudless, the ocean sparkling in the sun, but flat calm. Temperatures were in the mid fifties as we left the harbor at seven a.m., admiring the weather and views at the same time. A really fine Alaska summer morning. My regular, and his buddies were all about the same age, mid forties, or so. All in good physical condition and raring to

ALASKAN DEEP SEA FISH TALES

fish. The old man of the group, was quite frail and about seventy five to eighty years old. He was perky though, and full of optimism about the day, talking incessantly about his wish to catch a fish over one hundred pounds. He went on and on about the big ones that had almost been caught, but never a fish over one hundred. His son told me, his dad had been an avid fisherman in his younger years and had fished for many species and in quite a few exotic locales. We all swapped fishing stories and enjoyed the hour and a half run to the fishing area for that day.

Arriving at the grounds, we were set up to fish and baiting hooks, while marveling at the perfect conditions we had this day. We had begun to use Miya Epoch twelve volt electric reels on the charter recently, so I had to go through a simple orientation with them all about the use of the reels. Mainly these are made to assist you, not to be used as winches. They actually are equalizers, and elderly people really enjoy them. This was just fine with the old man. He feistily proposed a five dollar bet with the others. Five each on first fish, five on biggest fish, and five more on most poundage of fish. After a lot of good natured horsing around about the bet we were ready to fish.

It wasn't too long before the first bites started. The water was perfectly calm and we were able to detect the slightest touch to the bait. Fishing was relatively slow, with sometimes many minutes between bites.

ALASKAN DEEP SEA FISH TALES

Soon we had the first keeper fish aboard. One of the Son's buddies caught it. Then the second fish was aboard, and so on. During the entire morning the old man had not had a single fish take a bait. When the others started rummaging in the cooler for food and drinks, he steadfastly refused to stop fishing. He admonished, he wasn't going to miss that bite because he was feeding his face. The day wore on and the atmosphere aboard got quieter and quieter. Everyone was pulling for the old man to get his fish. One by one they all quit fishing as the day's catch added up. The fishing cockpit was still and quiet as we got closer to the regular quitting time. The weather and water remained perfect. No one suggested we quit, but they knew the day was getting towards its end. Still the old man fished on, more intent than ever. Still assuring everyone, he would get a fish. I was reaching a point of complete frustration. Everyone else had caught nice fish and done it relatively easily, why wouldn't the dumb fish bite the old mans bait? We repositioned the boat at the top of the drift I had been running all day. With fresh bait once again on the old mans hook, we collectively crossed our fingers and hoped.

At just about the time I was giving up completely, on seeing a fish, any fish take his bait, there was a tiny tug on the line. Then a more forceful tug! The old man didn't move, he wisely was waiting until he was sure the fish was on the bait. Another strong pull, and the reel drag started slipping. Now the fight was on, we had a real nice fish on his line and every soul on the boat was mentally fighting that fish along with the fisherman. After a long fight,

ALASKAN DEEP SEA FISH TALES

maybe forty or fifty minutes, he had the fish close to the boat and worn out enough so it was a simple job to shoot it and get it aboard. All one hundred and seventy five pounds of it. Total celebration broke out, we were all yelling and screaming congratulations at him and each other. It was total yahoo time. The old man was glowing from the excitement. He kept saying. "I told you I could do it. I knew I would catch one over a hundred." Everyone was super happy and we started making ready to start the long ride back to port.

As I was picking things up and stowing them, the old man came up to me and quietly asked. "Skipper do you think we could do one more down? This is probably going to be my last Halibut trip and after that fish, I feel lucky." I was as excited as anyone else was and thought what the heck. Okay we'll do one more ten minute down, just for you.

Again I repositioned the boat and let the old man lower a fresh bait to the bottom. The heavy lead hit the bottom. He flipped the drag forward to stop the free spool, and tightened the slack out of the line. As the slack tightened, there was a tremendous hit on the bait that almost jerked the rod out of his hands. He gamely fought it for a few minutes as the fish was running hard, then realizing he was exhausted from the first fish, passed the rod to his son. Beaming at everyone on the boat, he was the star of the hour. The second fish was fought by virtually all of the other fishermen then boated. It weighed one hundred and ninety two pounds.

ALASKAN DEEP SEA FISH TALES

The old man had got his fish. He won the betting pool for most pounds and biggest fish. Although there was a weak attempt to disqualify the second poundage, because it was a shared fish. Everyone was proud to have been a part of that day. It was one of the truly magic days we have now and then.

Turned out too, that was the old mans last Halibut trip. Sadly, he passed away the following year. But, his son said, he told a lot of happy stories about those big fish in the meantime.

ALASKAN DEEP SEA FISH TALES

ALASKAN DEEP SEA FISH TALES

AN INTERESTING FOURTH OF JULY

This particular fourth of July morning, dawned with a promise of rougher weather before the day was over. The bright early morning light showed through thin, high cirrus clouds and a fitful wind blowing out on the bay waters, in front of Seldovia. Even at this early hour, five-thirty, there were hints of whitecaps, where the wind was skirling the water.

I readied the boat as was normal. Standard procedure indicated we would take a look at the open ocean, at least, before giving up to threatening weather. By seven a.m. everything was ready to roll.

My crew for that day, were all Alaskan residents, from Anchorage. All were young to middle aged, and in top physical condition. Two of them had been on charter with me previously, two hadn't. they all showed up on schedule and were pleasantly agreeable to try the water even though it looked as if it was going to rough up. There was a small tide range for the day, that would help keep the wave size down some, if the wind velocity became strong.

We left the shelter of Seldovia Bay knowing it would be a relatively slow ride to the desired fishing area, with the swells above five feet and small whitecaps. The ride out was slower than normal cruise, but not too bad, eventually we reached our intended fishing area. Upon stopping the boat we were all pleased to find the water conditions reasonably livable, and commenced to rig up. No one was at all seasick. Great!

Fishing was slow and steady, we put some real nice fish on board, slower catching than I like to do, but the pressure was off. We would have an acceptable day of it, even if we got blown out later. The morning tide change helped calm the seas down. As the tide approached slack, the water calmed to about three or four foot seas, fifteen knots of wind.

All of the group were fishing steadily, talking and telling jokes with each other, generally having a good time. One of them broke into the conversation, telling me that he was hung up on the bottom. I responded, I didn't believe that was possible, due to the type of bottom we were fishing. Stepping over to him, I could see his rod was sharply bent and the drag was allowing line to spool out very slowly, classic signs of a snag on the bottom. Observing the rig for a few seconds, I decided he was hung up on something. I suggested he try to jerk it free, by yanking up hard on the rod, sometimes this will free up a kelp snag or a patch of mussels.

Winding the rod tip down to the water, he reefed back on the heavy ocean rod as hard as he could. No success, other

ALASKAN DEEP SEA FISH TALES

than the drag releasing a small amount of line. Winding the tip back down to the water again, he pulled up forcefully again. This time there was a response. The reel started screaming line out in the opposite direction. He was hooked up on a big momma Halibut, that had mouthed the bait then just laid there. Any other action we had taken, possibly would have caused the fish to just release the bait, instead she was hooked solidly.

For a long time he fought the fish, over an hour, and the big fish was still not at the boat. During the long fight, the weather had started to worsen. Seas were now over six feet and building, winds were gusting between twenty and twenty five knots, but the sun was still shining weakly. I had the gun out and the harpoon rigged and ready, with the toggle line tied off to a cleat. Finally the huge fish was showing color. About twenty feet down in the water, the fish looked to be three hundred or better, I told them. Excited is probably too mild a word to use about the conditions on the boat at this time. Everyone was charged with adrenaline.

I elected to harpoon the fish first, instead of shooting it, because of the roughening sea conditions. Once we had a solid harpoon tip in the fish we could manhandle it up and shoot it before bringing it aboard. If I shot it first, I was worried about losing it before I could gaff or harpoon it. Finally, after cautioning and re-cautioning the fishermen about the danger of becoming entangled in the quarter inch double braid nylon harpoon line, we were ready. The fish

ALASKAN DEEP SEA FISH TALES

broached the water totally flat and right beside the boat. I stabbed hard with the harpoon and felt the tip break out through the other side of the beautiful fish. Solid harpoon, we had it.

At about the same time I stabbed the fish, the heavily stressed dacron fishing line on the fisherman's rod, snapped at the upper swivel, just above the heavy mono leader. The fisherman who had fought it for so long panicked, thinking his huge fish was being lost. He literally threw the rod down into the boat and immediately grabbed the loose nylon line attached to the harpoon, wrapping the tough line around his wrist several times, without me noticing. I had picked up the gun and was preparing to shoot the fish, so we could board it.

Several things began to happen at once. The fish was coming out of its stupor, and realizing it was hurt, wanted to depart the area. I saw the fish arch in preparation of a powerful run, at the same time I was looking to be sure the harpoon line was not tangled, the fish would just slam against the end of the tied off line and after fighting the tension for a few minutes, be ready to give up. As I looked at the harpoon line I saw with horror, the line wrapped around the fisherman's wrist. Knowing instantly, he would be pulled overboard by the fish or have his hand torn off by the thin nylon line, I shouted in panic for him to get away from that line, NOW! He knew from the look on my face, I was scared, and tried to shake the coils loose. By now the

ALASKAN DEEP SEA FISH TALES

fish was in motion and gaining momentum every inch it moved.

Everything regarding time and motion slowed to ultra slow motion for me at this point. The fisherman had shaken the coils of line loose from his wrist, but I saw there was still a wad of tangled line on his wet fingers. The fish was now pulling the slack line, only about twenty feet, over the side, faster and harder, with a deadly sounding high pitched whirr, as the speed increased. In a millisecond the line was in a tight half-hitch on the fisherman's little finger. Watching helplessly as the two second drama took place, I saw the line go tight, then yank the fisherman's hand over the edge of the rail. In an instant the force had snapped off the end of my client's little finger. I felt sick as I watched the piece of finger hit the water and disappear.

He fell back to the deck, looking at his hand in stunned disbelief, along with all of the rest of us. Blood was pouring from his hand. My only thought was to get him ashore as quickly as possible, and I reached for the bait knife to cut the fish free of the boat. I was reaching out with the knife, when my client forcefully yelled out at me. "What the Hell are you doing?" He exclaimed. I told him I was cutting the fish loose so we could get back to town and medical attention. His response stopped me cold. "Don't you dare cut that fish loose, my hand is already hurt, at least we can still get the fish." Looking at the others I mentally shrugged and asked for assistance in shooting and landing the fish. We cautiously hand lined the big fish back up to the surface. I then shot it, ending the battle. In only a minute or two we had hauled it to the deck and, after doing minor first aid to the damaged finger, started running as hard as I dared in the heavy seas, back towards Seldovia. It was a rough and stressful ride back.

On the way in I radioed for medical help to be standing by at the harbor. Upon arriving the whole Seldovia paramedic team was waiting to assist. After they had done what they could to ease his pain and cleanse the injury, it was necessary to airlift him back to an Anchorage hospital for surgery on the hand.   He was flown back to Anchorage, had successful repair surgery on the finger and recovered completely. The fish weighed out at two hundred and eleven pounds. It did look a lot bigger in the water though.

ALASKAN DEEP SEA FISH TALES

DAD, OH MY GAWD!

For several years after I started chartering full time during the summer, my teenage daughter lived in Seldovia for the entire season, taking care of minor boat maintenance, bait prep and clean up, each day. There were days when she also went out as deck hand. This is one of those days.

The morning had begun with a storm warning being posted on the weather channel. The weather in Seldovia was not too bad, but the barometer was falling rapidly. The sky was heavily overcast, with fat black clouds promising heavy rains soon. Water conditions were not at all bad, with other charter boats reporting only two foot seas offshore, with light winds.

After discussing the situation thoroughly with the clients. We decided to get out, catch as many fish as possible before the storm hit, and start running for shore at the first sign of severe weather on the water. With boats already trying to fish the central inlet waters and reporting small seas, I figured we had a few hours at least before things got wild.

In the charter business you judge each day, by whether you can get the job done and the clients satisfied without undue

ALASKAN DEEP SEA FISH TALES

risk of injury or even death. Serious injury or worse is possible out on the water, nearly every day. A stormy day multiplies the risk, and it is something every charter boat skipper takes very seriously. Getting someone injured is an absolute no no, especially so in today's litigation oriented society. The pressure is always on every operator though, to get the booked clients out on schedule and catch the fish. The charter season in Alaska is short and intense. Once you scrap a day, you don't get a chance to make it up later. With all of these thoughts analyzed and filed, we left the harbor and started for the fishing grounds.

The ride out was not really too bad. The sky was unsettling with the ominous blackness of a storm approaching, but the seas were small. The water had an unfriendly black look to it, caused by the heavy overcast, but it was oily smooth and there was no wind. We reached the fishing area easily and were convinced things were going to be a piece of cake.

Fishing was phenomenal, we started nailing beautiful fish one after another, fish were averaging sixty pounds or better and were taking the bait quickly and solidly. We were two fish short of a boat limit, about two hours after we had started to fish, when the first warning gusts of wind swept across the boat.

Swells, open ocean waves, with no crests, had started building a short time earlier, with the tide switch, but were not threatening at all. We decided to do one more drift

ALASKAN DEEP SEA FISH TALES

over the drop off we were fishing, then call it a day. We made the drift, caught the two fish we needed and stowed things for the run in. My daughter was washing down the decks, clearing them of the slippery slime from the fish. I was high fiveing the clients for doing so well and everything was satisfactory as I started the boat engines.

I noticed as I turned towards Seldovia the building swells, now about eight feet with a little fringe of white foam on top, and the increasing winds were coming out of the Northwest, unusual but reassuring to me because, in my experiences, this would mean they would not build too high, as they were not coming into the bay from the open ocean. My daughter finished the outside chores and entered the damp but warm cabin, commenting to me about her unease with the still growing swells. I was talking to her about the changing weather conditions when the radio started giving reports of severe seas Northwest of our position. Some of the Homer boats were encountering very large seas and wind, all of them were running for shelter. I was a little rattled by the reports, but I didn't feel we would have to battle through any terrible water to reach port. We would be moving Easterly and should stay ahead of the approaching disturbance. I also felt the reports were being slightly exaggerated, because of the storm warning.

We ran about five or six miles towards shore before the skies opened up with a deluge. It was raining cats and dogs outside. The boat wipers would barely allow me to see a path directly ahead of our course, and black water was

ALASKAN DEEP SEA FISH TALES

mostly all I saw. I had my daughter position herself on the forward left side of the cabin so she could watch the water on that side of the boat. The big swells were coming from that direction and I needed to watch the course as we made headway. With her eyes to the left I could quarter into the seas with more confidence. The fishermen had all become quiet.

The wind had steadily increased and was now blowing at least forty knots. Rain was sluicing down sideways and incredibly the swells continued to grow, now becoming menacing waves at the crest. It was noon and the light outside was that of twilight, only with a greenish cast. I had never seen conditions change this severely this quickly in the central inlet before and was becoming concerned. The seas were now topping fourteen feet by my estimation, and still building higher. My thirty foot boat was being tossed like a cork from crest to trough, and back again. At times I was having a problem keeping the boat positioned properly to keep it from broaching sideways in the monstrous mountains of water we were now encountering. We were still making good headway though and I knew if we could get far enough East into the Bay, we would be sheltered by the outcrop of land at Anchor Point.

I told my daughter to start rating the waves for me so I could anticipate how much to steer into the wave front as we rode up the face. Since I couldn't see the approaching seas. Big would be the average, bigger would naturally be just that, and really big Dad, would mean a strong course

ALASKAN DEEP SEA FISH TALES

correction as the wave struck. This system was working fine as we continued to be slapped and pounded around. At no time did the boat feel out of control, nor did I feel really threatened, just concerned. The seas continued to enlarge. Sixteen then eighteen feet. Bigger and really big became normal. All at once my daughter shouted. Really, really big one Dad, be careful. She had no more than said this when she said. Dad! Oh my Gawd. I slammed the wheel over hard in her direction to bring the bow into the wave more. As the vision area in the windshield came around I saw, with total open mouthed terror, the biggest wave I have ever encountered in Cook Inlet. It was a rogue wave, spaced further apart than the pattern had been, but at least thirty feet high and cresting in the near distance up ahead. In the short time I had before the wave got to us, all I could do is look at it in complete awe. A mountain of water was bearing down on us and there was no way to avoid it. The face of it looked to be fifty or sixty degrees off of level, steepening as you approached the crest. We Started up the face at a relatively smooth spot and I hoped we would top out before the cresting action reached where we were at. If that breaking crest hit us broadside it could, probably would, swamp the boat easily. There were untold tons of water moving off the top of this unbelievable wave jutting out of the ocean. I yelled for everyone to hang on and gritted my teeth as we started up this overwhelming wall of water. In only a few seconds we topped the face of the wave, at the same time, the cresting part got to us, and for a few seconds there was no visibility at all, only crashing water and the boat moving forcefully in unpredictable directions. Coming off the back side of the wave I looked back out of the cabin and could see water at least a foot deep in the fishing cockpit, but we were still afloat and the engines never missed a beat. The clients stated, they were completely impressed, but could we please go home now. My feelings exactly. My daughter remained silent.

Gratefully within a very few minutes after the huge rogue wave hit, we were feeling the seas start to diminish, we had made the protection of the bluff at Anchor Point. The rest of the trip in was uneventful. The seas were off of our stern now and much smaller than before. After docking, back in Seldovia we found out that two other boats had windshields knocked out in the sudden fury. One of the boats damaged was over fifty feet in length.

All of the clients thought we had a great adventure. I knew we had experienced a very close call.

ALASKAN DEEP SEA FISH TALES

HIGH EXPECTATIONS

We get a variety of fishermen and women in our business. These people come from all walks of life, and from all points of the world. Some would be satisfied to catch anything at all, others want to get a trophy fish, still others are up in Alaska just for the enjoyment of being in a place many people never get the privilege of seeing. In the charter business you eventually get to see most all types. This is one of the things that make chartering a fun and intensely interesting way to spend the summer months. To be successful as a charter skipper you must like people and the challenges, as well as the satisfactions, they produce each day. The lifetime fantasy of one fisherman can be a ho hum deal for another.

The group of scheduled clients this day were a foursome from Oregon. All were young men in their twenties. I would say they were typical young, upwardly mobile business people, up to have a fishing experience to tell their friends about back home. They had said upon arrival they wanted to catch good fish, but above all they wanted to catch lots of fish. I had assured them the fish had been running strong, and we had been getting fish in the hundred pound class quite regularly. They didn't seem either

ALASKAN DEEP SEA FISH TALES

impressed or disappointed with my description of the fishing.

After all of the routine stuff and introductions we made the trip out, nearly thirty miles on this trip. It was a perfect post card day with ideal conditions and visibility. The kind of day you always see in the pictures on the brochures. Indescribable scenery, glass flat water. I just knew we were going to have a day to remember. The four clients asked all of the routine questions, asked by each and every novice to Alaska. I tried to answer all their questions and told fish stories on the smooth trip out. Arriving on site, we were the only boat in sight. How good can it get?

I instructed all of them with the gear and we were soon lowering bait to the bottom, two hundred feet below. As the first hook hit bottom, it was immediately picked up by a large fish, surprising the new angler quite badly. After a few moments of chaos we got things under control, and settled down for the long fight. While the one client was working, what I knew to be a very good fish, I had all of the others bring in their lines and stand by.

The fish made long runs several times, seemingly frustrating the client, I kept telling him to enjoy the action, that's what they were here for. He wanted the fish in the boat though, and each time the fish ran, he became more agitated. After a quite prolonged battle we finally boated the fish. A tremendous fish too, two hundred and thirty eight pounds, a super fish by my standards. The clients all

ALASKAN DEEP SEA FISH TALES

thought it was a pretty nice way to start the day, but were still surprisingly not too excited.

I was personally pumped up good. A two thirty plus fish on the first down, and the whole day in front of us. I was also puzzled by their actions. A fish that large usually merits a large celebration. I moved the boat back to the drift area where we had hooked the big fish.

It wasn't very long and we had another very fine fish on one of the lines. It fought well and hard, but we boated it without too much hassle. Now I'm really happy. The second fish was about eighty five or ninety pounds. Over three hundred pounds of fish aboard in only two fish. What a day we had going. Kneeling over the newly boated fish I looked up at the fishermen and was really baffled. They weren't even excited, not at all. Here I am having my own personal party, about a hundred times happier than the guys paying for the trip. Something was wrong, I suddenly worried that I had done something to offend them, either on the way out or with instructions, or something. I couldn't imagine for the life of me, what it could have been though.

I repositioned the boat on the drift for the third time and announced, we were ready to fish again. When I came out of the cabin, they hadn't yet started to lower their lines. I was now certain there was something wrong, so I asked them if there was a problem with anything. Well, no, nothing was wrong, but they wanted to know if we were going to continue to keep all the little fish that were hooked.

I was speechless, something not usual with me. I finally asked. "What little fish? We haven't caught any little fish." The lead man of the group pointed over at the second fish, laying on the deck. "Those little fish." He said, kind of offhandedly. "We came up to Alaska to catch big fish. I don't want to keep anything smaller than the first one." For a few seconds I thought my heart had stopped, I was so stunned. For someone to expect a two hundred plus pound fish to be the smallest fish of the day was unthinkable.

Calling a time out, I started to question them about how they had come to think catching fish that large was commonplace. After several minutes of conversation, a picture emerged. They had received brochures from numerous charter operations in several different areas of the State, and virtually all of them showed nothing but two and three hundred pound fish. They had assumed this was the common fish to be landed. I had to vigorously explain to them that the first fish aboard was most likely, the largest fish we would see, and it was a once in a lifetime event for most people to catch one that big. We then continued to fish and ended the day with a super load. Our smallest fish was about sixty five pounds. After getting back to the harbor and showing them what some of the other boats were bringing in, they cheered up somewhat

ALASKAN DEEP SEA FISH TALES

and seemed satisfied when they left Seldovia. However, I have never heard from any of this group again.

This trip is one of the prime reasons I decided to never plaster my advertising brochures with any pictures of very large fish. They are not an everyday occurrence, and should be highly appreciated when they are caught.

ALASKAN DEEP SEA FISH TALES

ALASKAN DEEP SEA FISH TALES

THE ENCOUNTER

Every once in a while, I get to see something on the ocean, I have never seen before. After nearly thirty years fishing Kachemak Bay and the Inlet, I still get surprised quite regularly. The ocean Is a strange and sometimes almost mystical place. This encounter took place in July of 1998. It is documented with many photographs.

I had left Seldovia with six clients on board, and a deck hand. We were all excited to be out and running, because the forecast had not been very encouraging the evening before, but the morning had begun beautifully. This group of customers were from out of State, and were looking forward to a fun day.

We had cleared Adam Point and were heading toward Elizabeth Island. Absolutely calm water with only a bare riffle of breeze on it. Bright sunshine on the sparkling sea and the clean smell of the ocean in the air. The outside air was cool and crisp, as it can be in mid July.

Some distance ahead I saw several whales spouting and broaching on the surface. Nearing the site, I saw there were many whales in the area. We counted between forty and fifty, in sight at any given time, and as many as sixteen

ALASKAN DEEP SEA FISH TALES

spouting simultaneously. This is unusual but it does happen, the clients were in a high state of excitement, encouraging me to try approaching more closely. I did so and found, to my surprise, these whales were as curious about us, as we were about them. Nearing the pod of whales I identified them as Humpbacks, a rather large variety of whale. I am presently running a thirty four foot boat, with a thirteen foot beam. Some of these magnificent creatures were longer than the boat and as wide. We approached to within fifty yards or so, behind the pods direction of travel.

I stopped the engines after placing the gearboxes in neutral. Letting the boat drift forward under its own momentum. What happened next was and still is, hard to believe. Two of the whales separated from the group and swam directly to the boat. As we watched in delight and indescribable pleasure. They passed under and around the boat several times, coming nearer each time. Soon they were literally brushing the boat with their huge bodies, causing some mild concern by everyone aboard. It was more than obvious, these great creatures could smash the boat to splinters in a second, if they desired to do so. The boat was gently touched and rocked slightly, but the touches were so gentle, it was plain these giant citizens of the sea were not intending damage or harm.

Everyone aboard was taking pictures like crazy, thinking the whales would disappear in a few more seconds. They didn't disappear at all, they became even more curious,

ALASKAN DEEP SEA FISH TALES

hanging in the water and touching the rudders and props with their flippers. Soon there was no more film aboard and we all stood in absolute astounded awe at what happened next. One of the whales approached the boat on the surface of the water, sticking up a foot or two out of the water. When it was literally at the side of the boat with its nose, it pushed its head into the water and passed under the fishing deck area of the boat, barely clearing the hull and in full sight of everyone, to display its entire length in the clear water. We were by now babbling at each other to have seen such a sight, only a couple of feet away. This was the most incredible whale encounter I had ever had, and the best was yet to come. My clients were nearly in pleasurable hysterics with what they were seeing.

After many loud cries about the shortage of film aboard, we continued to watch the antics of the two whales. They were not in the slightest, afraid or intimidated by the boat or our shouts of pleasure, as they performed their movements. Thirty minutes went by and the whales were still touching and examining the boat from all angles and all directions. There were many times during this period it would have been possible to step from the boat to a whales back with absolutely no difficulty. How long you could have stayed there is another question, but that is how close they were to us.

After many passes under and around the boat, one of the whales positioned itself off of the left or port side of the boat, facing forward and floating quite high out of the

ALASKAN DEEP SEA FISH TALES

water. The sun was glistening off of its dark surface, and you could see clearly, masses of barnacles and sea growths on its body. The whale kept easing closer and closer to the boat, sculling the water with its huge flippers. When it was only a few feet from the side, it started to roll over on its back, still moving closer to the side of the boat. As it reached the boat, it sunk slowly into the water, upside down and touched the windows on the left side, with its ten foot long flipper. Continuing, it rolled completely under the boat with the flipper tip still against the windows, then slowly rolled out the other side of the boat. Incredulous, we all stood there silently for a second or two then broke out in cheers. The boat had been hugged by a whale! Unbelievable but true. This giant, gentle behemoth had touched the boat and rolled completely under it without as much as rocking it. Surfacing on the right side it blew loudly and swam off from us. The absolute control these creatures have over their bodies is beyond astounding.

This action seemed to be a signal of goodbye, because in only a little while the two whales were swimming smoothly and steadily away back to the larger group still nearby. We sat there for awhile, enjoying the gorgeous morning while discussing what had just happened. The mutual feelings of all aboard were the same. We had just had a near religious experience. The feelings of wonder and joy we all had, to have been privileged to see this magnificent display, were nearly indescribable. That day will be in my personal memory banks until I die.

ALASKAN DEEP SEA FISH TALES

We eventually went on to the fishing grounds and had a very nice day. But everyone was talking and thinking about the whales for the whole time.

ALASKAN DEEP SEA FISH TALES

ALASKAN DEEP SEA FISH TALES

THE FEMALE PHILOSOPHY

Being a male individual and having lived for several decades, I realize those of the female gender sometimes look at life differently than males. This short story is about how totally differently that can be.

Occasionally I book groups of all female fishermen. I enjoy taking all female trips for several different reasons. One, what guy wouldn't enjoy being in charge, on a boat full of women? Just joking. Usually the groups of women are aggressive in wanting to catch fish. This will prove to their husbands and boyfriends that females can catch fish.

Mostly what I hear from these ladies is this. They want to fish their way. They don't want to be criticized on their fishing style or form. They don't want to be yelled at when they lose a fish. Most women really don't want to compete directly against a male fisherman. When they do fish with men friends, they get all of the above.

In many instances, I can verify, if a woman is fishing with her significant other, and catches the biggest fish, she gets hassled about it not complimented. This is observation from many trips, guys, on my part, so you might consider a more positive attitude next time she gets the big one.

ALASKAN DEEP SEA FISH TALES

My charter trips that have been all female have varied from everyday housewives, to business associates, to a group of neighborhood friends, to once, a foursome of topless dancers from one of the Anchorage Clubs.

The most common thread running through all of the trips is, the women groups are almost always more mellow than the guys. Women mostly don't do macho. They want to catch fish, but they would rather gossip than tell put down stories. They talk about the kids, and their other half. They are willing to work as a team immediately. And I have never ever seen a woman pick on another woman who got seasick. Something men do all the time.

This day, there were four job associated ladies aboard, they all worked for the same company in Anchorage. Their ages ranged from early twenties to mid forties. One of them was a really petite woman who couldn't have weighed much over a hundred pounds, if that. Everyone was immune to seasickness, they had all fished the ocean before. A good thing because it was going to be somewhat rough. Scattered rain showers, with building wind and seas in the afternoon was the forecast.

We mutually agreed to fish the upper portion of the Bay, between Seldovia and Anchor Point. This would keep us out of the potentially really rough water south of English Bay. They just wanted to have a good day and bring back some fish.

ALASKAN DEEP SEA FISH TALES

We arrived on the fishing hole without incident and commenced fishing. The seas were about three feet, the weather gray and chilly. Occasionally we got rained on but everyone aboard was landing Halibut regularly. We started to build a decent load in the fish boxes, and the mood among them was jovial. After several drifts the fishing got slower then stopped. I should say catching got slower then stopped. The ladies didn't quit. After some time with no bites at all I suggested we move the boat to another ledge and try again. Everyone was agreeable to this.

While I ran the boat to the next spot, the clients all used the time to dry out while warming up a little and eat a sandwich or two. Gossiping happily among themselves as we ran, they were happy with the day so far. Arriving at the second ledge, everyone was refreshed and ready to get at it again.

We started fishing right at the tide change, and things were fairly slow, but showed promise. As the incoming tide started to pick up velocity, I had to move the boat regularly to keep us fishing where I wanted to. On this run I decided to move the boat further into deeper water so we would have a longer drift and be on the bottom longer before hitting the top of the ledge. Weather conditions were staying about the same as we had, to start the day with.

After setting the baits on the bottom of this deeper water, it wasn't long before we had a really big fish on. The tiny

49

petite gal had one that wouldn't budge. For some time I wasn't positive it was a fish or a snag, but eventually it made a run and then there was no doubt. She turned into a tiger with that fish. It would run and she would stubbornly reel back. She wouldn't let anyone else touch the rod. She was going to catch this one all by herself or else. The fight went on for a very long time. The other ladies had stopped fishing when this one was hooked and formed a support group around the small lady. They brought her something to drink, rubbed her shoulders, offered to help wind the reel, and offered tons of advise and encouragement.

Eventually the fish was visible in the darkness below the boat. I knew it was large, while she was fighting it, but hadn't expected it to be the size it was. The Halibut she had was very honestly, the largest halibut I have ever seen. As she brought it to the surface, an inch at a time, it looked bigger and bigger. When she eased it closer to the surface, I was going nuts, I started telling all of them what would have to be done to boat it, and I was frantic that we might lose it. One of the other ladies looked over and saw the fish, then quietly went into the cabin. The lady with the fish on finally saw what she had and was exultant. The other two were just standing there staring at this gigantic Halibut. This fish was easily nine to ten feet long, and four to five feet wide. A monster! Easily over four hundred pounds.

Before I could try to harpoon or shoot the fish, she turned to me and said. "I don't want to kill it, I caught it, I know

ALASKAN DEEP SEA FISH TALES

I caught it, that's all that matters, let it go." There was instantaneous agreement from the rest of the crew. In fact there was celebration from the rest of them. I futilely tried to argue the positives of bringing in a fish that big, but they were adamant. Let it go. All of this became academic about this time, because the big fish had become aware it wasn't where it was suppose to be. It made one shake of its head and flipped the hook out. Then serenely sank slowly back into the dark ocean.

The group couldn't have been more happy if we had landed two fish that size. They had proven to themselves they were capable of bringing up a big fish, and they didn't need a carcass to show anyone. We finished out the day and had an exuberant ride back to the dock.

I don't know of any male fisherman who would have done what they did. There may be a few, in today's conservation oriented world , but I feel there are very few men, myself included, who would be willing to turn back a fish that size.

ALASKAN DEEP SEA FISH TALES

ALASKAN DEEP SEA FISH TALES

FLY FISHING FOR HALIBUT-ALMOST

Halibut are well known for their bottom hugging activities, but there are times when they are anywhere but, on the bottom. In all the years I've fished Halibut, I have seen them gathered on the surface only three times. This was one of them.

My clients and I had been fishing the area of Kachemak Bay, known in the charter business as the South Ledge. We were having a terrible time of it this particular day. The weather was pretty nice, the water was smooth, but the fish were just not willing to bite. I had been fishing this spot for many days and I had not experienced any problems landing fish, until today. We had used up most of the scheduled fishing time and only landed a couple of barely keeper sized fish. Not a good thing for a skipper to have happening.

The clients were regular clients, they had been out many times before with me, and had experienced good fishing. None of us could remember such a poor day, with such good conditions. In frustration, I suggested we move to a spot several miles away, and give it our best shot, in the fishing time left. They all agreed, it couldn't be much worse than what we had going. So off we went.

53

ALASKAN DEEP SEA FISH TALES

While under way I nearly always watch the sonar or depth sounder, at least glance at it regularly, as we are moving. Sometimes you can pick up indications of fish or interesting structure as you run. I have found numerous good fishing spots over the years, this way.

On this day as we were running over virtually flat bottom, according to the sonar, I was noticing indications of very large balls of bait fish in the mid water levels. I commented on this to the fishermen and they became additionally interested in these indicators. They were all avid fishermen and knew how to read sonar signals, soon we were all talking about the intensity of the return signals we were getting. On the screen, big red orange blobs were showing seventy five to a hundred feet below. This indicates a nearly solid mass of biomass, on my equipment.

Soon we saw the masses were showing up closer to the surface, then nearly beneath the boat. This was too much for our curiosity, so we stopped the boat to take a look. We all went out on the deck and stared into the green ocean water. At first we couldn't see anything unusual, but as we kept looking, we were soon seeing movement, some feet below the boat. After some time of trying to figure out the vague shadows below, someone suddenly yelled that it was Halibut. It was, thousands and thousands of Halibut, ranging from five pounds to fish well in excess of a hundred pounds. We quickly lowered baits down a few feet, we could clearly see the sinkers and hooks. No

ALASKAN DEEP SEA FISH TALES

interest from the milling fish. They seemed to see the bait, but had no interest in it. Now we are really wound up tight. Thousands of fish visible, but they won't take a hook, what to do. While watching the slow stately movements of the masses of fish, one of the fishermen took a chunk of bait and threw it several yards away from the boat. The instant it hit the water, there was action, dozens of fish swam towards it immediately and fought each other to get at it. Again we threw several bait chunks in the water, fish zoomed in on them, and sucked the pieces down, actually biting each other to try for the drifting baits.

We hastily removed the lead weights from our gear and baited the hooks generously. Then unspooling several yards of line we coiled it and flung the non-weighted gear over the side. Within a few minutes the bait had created a feeding frenzy on the surface and just beneath the surface. A huge mass of Halibut were around and under the boat competing for every scrap of bait they could find. Fish were striking, and fishermen were vying for the bigger fish. Trying to keep the bait from the smaller fish, and let a bigger one take it. It got to be a big game.

Fish were being hooked on every line. With no weights on the lines, the action was indescribable. Halibut were flying out of the water trying to shake hooks out, the water was literally boiling with fish on the surface. Lines were going in all directions. Insanity! It was like fishing in a hatchery pond that hadn't been fed in a week.

ALASKAN DEEP SEA FISH TALES

One fisherman had shouted for me to gaff a fish that was at the boat. In the maelstrom of action, I reached over and gaffed a forty plus pound fish and pulled it aboard, only to find out it had been a freely swimming fish, the fisherman's fish was still hooked up, in the water. Who ever heard of free gaffing Halibut on the open ocean.

We continued this fishing until we had boated our limits. I don't know how many we had released during the frenzy, but it was in the many dozens. After we stopped fishing there were still hundreds of Halibut slowly swimming around in the water. It was a real neat experience.

I have only seen this activity a few times and find it unexplainable. The Halibut, when they are this way, are not skittish at all. They seem to be almost in a daze, and don't react to much of anything until a meal hits the water. Another of the mysteries of the sea.

Every time you think you have seen all of the sights you can see on the ocean, I personally guarantee, the ocean will throw something at you that will take your breath away.

ALASKAN DEEP SEA FISH TALES

THE SUMMER FROM HELL!

With the beginning of each charter season, every operator knows there will be some days that are more trying than others. We all know that some mechanical failures will occur, and we all try our utmost to prevent these things from happening, as much as possible. Pre-season preventative maintenance is high on every skippers list.

Many of our customers think we have the greatest job in the world. Us skippers get to go fishing every day! Sorry to disappoint you guys. We get to go out on the boat each day. We get to share the fun and different experiences. We get to be part of once in a lifetime memories. All of these do make chartering a great way to spent the summer. We don't get to go fishing, hardly ever.

We also get to stay up all night fixing a broken boat, or piece of vital equipment. Sometimes literally, all night, and then get to go out again, if we're lucky, the next morning. These are the times when you question your sanity for doing this.

Dead tired, after an all night repair session, you greet the clients with a smile. They have planned this day for many months, and they have every right to expect things as they

ALASKAN DEEP SEA FISH TALES

should be. They don't ever want to hear, Sorry, my boat is broken. Sometimes, that's all you can say, but most skippers or boat owners will understand the following tale, of the summer my daughter and I remember as, The Summer From Hell.

We launched our boat in early May that year. Excited because we had repowered the boat with brand new engines, and had the transmissions rebuilt, while the boat was torn apart. The new engines performed nicely on the test runs. I was sure we had mechanical problems solved for this summer for sure.

The season started very well, and for a few trips everything was great. After about thirty hours on the brand new engines, I was noticing an alarming increase in oil usage, a quart or more each day on each engine. Conferring with the company that had sold me the engines, for a huge sum of money, I was told to just run them a little harder for a few days, The piston rings probably hadn't seated in right. A day or two of hard running would probably cure the situation. The next trip I increased the R.P.M. on the engines by about ten percent, as advised. Within an hour one engine had blown up, the other was running at about one tenth of its normal power. Bad deal, but as the saying goes, stuff happens.

We pulled the boat out of the water at Seldovia, our home port, yanked the engines out, and flew them back to Anchorage. The engine shop promised a rush analysis on the problems, a quick repair and we would be okay.

ALASKAN DEEP SEA FISH TALES

After three days of run-around and non-answers, I was becoming extremely agitated to say the least. Finally the engine people agreed to replace the ruined, brand new, engines, with rebuilt engines. This caused me great grief as you can imagine. I had bought brand new, so I wouldn't have problems with rebuilt. Much conversation later we had the rebuilt engines on a plane back to Seldovia, late one afternoon. Working all night long, my daughter and I installed the replacement engines and had the boat running and in the water two hours before the booked clients were supposed to go fishing. Yahoo! We were back on track.

Just before I reached the fishing grounds on the first run out, I got a low oil indicator warning light on the port engine. Stopping the boat and checking the engine, I found extremely low oil. I was baffled but refilled the engine sump from stock on board, and we had our day of fishing. On the way in, I got an low oil signal again, just as we entered the harbor. Checking the engine confirmed low oil. I found all the oil in the bilge of the boat. After much hassle and bad words, we had pulled the engine out two more times and taken it to Anchorage, before the engine shop figured out they had installed the rear main bearing cap with a metal burr on it, causing all the oil to push out of the rear seal.

Back to Seldovia again, for another all night session. The next morning we were ready to run again, after the third all nighter in less than a week of agony. We left the harbor on time and as I accelerated the boat to speed at the mouth of the Bay, the right engine gave a huge crash, and stopped. We had broken the crankshaft on that engine.

After a gigantic fight with the engine people, they agreed to have the engine fixed in forty eight hours. Great, another all nighter putting this engine back in. They did fix it, in the time frame they said, and we installed it, working through the night to do so.

By now you probably know, my sense of humor was black, to say the least. I had spent thousands of dollars to prevent exactly what was happening! Frustrated, dead tired, and more than a little apprehensive. I left the harbor once again, to try and make at least one full day without problems. Five engine change outs in less than two weeks. I couldn't even imagine having to change engines in that boat again.

Amazingly we ran fine, one day, two days, then a week went by. I was happy again. Perseverance pays off, we had stuck it out and things were going to be great. WRONG!

I had spent the previous day doing full scheduled maintenance on the new, rebuilt, repaired, and re-repaired engines. Changed oil and filters, checked everything out from top to bottom. Satisfied that things were in order I got ready for the next days trip.

ALASKAN DEEP SEA FISH TALES

We left the harbor in good spirits, a nice day, clients that had been out before and knew of my trials over the last couple of weeks. There was some good natured joking about life jackets and that sort of thing, but I was undeterred, the boat was fixed. Running out, I kept hearing funny noises from the engines. Everyone said I was imagining it, the engines sounded great. I convinced myself I was shell shocked and continued to run the boat. All the gauges were in the green, its okay. At this point the port engine totally blew up. WHAM!, end of discussion. We opened the engine compartment and saw the engine was destroyed. There was shrapnel all over and pieces of internal parts sticking out of it.

Totally despondent, I decided to try and fish the clients, before starting back on one engine. We fished and caught fish, although I can't say I was very pleasant to be with that day. We ran slowly back in towards Seldovia on one engine. I was sweating bullets all the way, fearing the other engine would quit, but it didn't. It waited to lock up as I was entering the harbor.

I decided to give up on the engine company. I bought two new engines from another dealer in Anchorage. Off road heavy duty, guaranteed to do the job engines, for another six thousand dollars. We flew the new engines to the boat, pulled the broken engines out with the dock crane.

By this time my personality was something close to Godzilla. My daughter, who had suffered as much sleep

ALASKAN DEEP SEA FISH TALES

deprivation as I, during this, was twitching and cringing every time I opened my mouth. I had started a lawsuit against the first supplier, and was threatening to do so to the new supplier, and I hadn't even put this set of new engines in the boat yet.

After hours and hours of miserable back breaking work I was totally ready to sink the boat and forget ever fishing again. We had taken the broken engines out to the airport and loaded them in the plane, brought the new engines down, installed all of the accessory stuff and were ready to do it again. My daughter was in the boat, twenty feet below the dock, to guide the engines into place as I lowered them on to the engine mounts. I told her to stand clear of the path before I started lowering the cradle cabled engine down with the crane.

She went into the boat cabin, and I started slowly lowering the brand new, never been started, engine down. About ten feet above the boat I suddenly had this overpowering urge to just push the free-spool on the winch controls and send the engine through the bottom of the boat. I stopped the winch and let the engine hang in the air over the back of my boat, turning slowly around and around.

My daughter, perceptive person that she is, sensed what I was considering doing and stepped out on the back deck. Actually placing herself beneath the several hundred pounds of hanging steel. Looking up at me, she wagged her finger, and said. "Dad, don't even think about it. I mean it. Don't even think of doing it." Then she started laughing. We discussed the pros and cons for a few minutes and went back to doing, what we knew, we had to do. Numerous hours later the boat was functional once again, and we ran for the next two years without any engine trouble. The summer was an interesting lesson in continuing on in the face of overwhelming defeats. There are times I wonder how I didn't just give up that year, but it all worked out. I lost many thousands of dollars that year and only recovered half of my costs from the sued engine company. My daughter and I ended that summer closer emotionally, than we had ever been. We still have a laugh or two occasionally about the seven engine summer.

I made an agreement with myself that year to never own another boat with gasoline engines, only diesels. I broke that agreement, once, and regretted it immediately. But that's another whole story.

ALASKAN DEEP SEA FISH TALES

ALASKAN DEEP SEA FISH TALES

FISH & GAME??

Years ago when regulations were much more relaxed than they are today, it was not uncommon for many sports fishermen to ignore published bag limits when ocean fishing. This was especially true if the fishing being done was more than twenty five miles offshore. For a time, there wasn't even a consensus among enforcement agency's in Alaska, as to the legal requirements of licensing sport fishing in the ocean. This was some time ago though, and there are rigid rules about every aspect of fishing on the ocean today.

This fine day I had six people on board, all middle aged men all out of Anchorage. Two of the fishermen I knew well. The other four were booked separately, and the two groups put together to make one full boat booking.

We were fishing well offshore, nearly thirty five miles out in the Gulf of Alaska. It was a perfect day, sunshine and blue sky, so blue it was almost purple. The water of the ocean was perfectly flat. It was warm enough to be fishing in just shirtsleeves, a really uncommon happening. The mountains one hundred miles away looked like movie scenes staged perfectly.

ALASKAN DEEP SEA FISH TALES

Fishing was beyond phenomenal, there are not words available to me to adequately describe how good things were this day. This day was your wildest fishing fantasy come true. Every time we put a hook on the bottom a great fish gobbled up the bait.

We started out right after arriving by simultaneously hooking three fish in the fifty pound range. Since it was right at the start of the day, we decided to keep one of them and throw the other two back. Everyone was having a great time and there was a common feeling on the boat, this would be one day to remember.

Fishing continued to improve as the morning went by. We had started out tossing fifty pounders, then sixties, finally we were regularly tossing seventy and eighty pound fish over the side. The fishing action was non-stop with fish on every line, every time a set of baits were lowered to the bottom. Every once in a while someone would say, keep that one, and I would cut its gills, then put it in the storage boxes. By lunch time we had an enormous load of fish in the boat, and were one fish short of legal boat limit. I was in ecstasy, and the clients were too.

Everyone decided to take a break, eat a sandwich, drink a beer or two, then try for another fish over one hundred and call it a day. We all talked about the incredible situation we were experiencing all by ourselves out in the middle of nowhere. Not one person in the group claimed to have ever had a Halibut trip even close to this good. We

ALASKAN DEEP SEA FISH TALES

finished eating, then I moved the boat back to the co-ordinates we had been working, and we lowered four sets of fresh bait down into the deep water.

Very soon after hitting bottom, one of the guys had a nice fish on, but he knew it wasn't big enough for this day and told everyone so. As he was fighting this fish, the other three fishermen hooked up, one, two, three good big fish on. All of them were telling each other, they had the biggest one, and they were all big fish, it was plain to see. We now had four fish working. One partially up to the boat we knew was a throwback, and three others, we were all curious about. We landed and released the first fish, only about sixty pounds, wow, another 'little' fish. There are many days I would give my teeth, for any of these 'little ones' we were throwing back.

After the normal tangles, runs and excitement that three big fish at once can give you, we finally got the first one to the surface. It was well over a hundred and the fisherman who caught it said, yes lets keep it. While the other two continued to work their fish, I shot and gaffed this one and drug it out of the water and into the boat. I had no more than finished with it, and a second one was at the side. Lots of activity was taking place at the same time.

I saw immediately that this fish was hurt badly, it had swallowed the big circle hook past its gullet. During the fight to the surface, the hook had torn through and into the gills. The fish was bleeding badly, and I knew it would not

ALASKAN DEEP SEA FISH TALES

survive. Without comment I shot and landed this fish, another well over a hundred.

Now we're one fish over limit, commented one of the anglers. I acknowledged this, and turned back to the last fisherman, still working his fish. When it reached the surface, we saw yet another big fish over a hundred. I told the fisherman, I was sorry but I was going to release it without lifting it out of the water, after what had just happened, I didn't want to risk injuring another one.

I worked the hook out of its jaw while hanging over the side of the boat, and we all cheered in a salute, when the fish swam swiftly off into the deeps.

Starting to organize the blood splattered deck in preparation for the trip home, I was not overly concerned about being one fish over limit. We were many miles offshore and the fish had been severely wounded. I don't believe in waste, and the situation was fully justified in my mind.

There were one or two comments made about being over limit, in a joking manner. I responded to these comments in a rather cavalier tone of voice, being extremely satisfied with the magnificent day. "One fish over isn't going to be a problem guys, after all no one here works for Fish and Game anyway." This was greeted by nods from two fishermen and silence from four fishermen.

ALASKAN DEEP SEA FISH TALES

I walked into the cabin to start the engines, my cocky confidence suddenly slightly uneasy, while my group of four fishermen had a quiet conference on the back deck. As I started the boat in motion, they entered the cabin. Without comment they all reached into their shirt pockets and showed me their badges and ID. All four worked for Fish and Game.

There were a few seconds when the thoughts I was having weren't printable. As they stood there, not smiling, with the multiple badges visible, I thought to myself, well you're busted, it's too late to be sorry now. I managed to smile weakly and tell them. "I don't feel any different than I did, I still would have kept the injured fish."

For a few more heartbeats, they maintained their severe composure, then started laughing all at once. After the big laugh was over they assured me, they were all just out on a fishing trip and the circumstances were acceptable to them individually and personally. We had numerous laughs at my expense on the way in. One of them told me, the look on my face was priceless when they showed their badges. I'm sure it was. My other two fishermen, had looked more than a little strange too!

ALASKAN DEEP SEA FISH TALES

ALASKAN DEEP SEA FISH TALES

THE UNEXPECTED CAN HAPPEN

Many times we look back on things that have happened in different parts of our past life, and wonder how those particular circumstances came together to cause an incident. The most innocuous items can add up to a significant event in any of our lives, at the most unexpected of times. This is about one of those significant happenings, in my life as a charter boat skipper.

The day started out as routinely as any day possibly could, the weather was good, fishing was expected to be great, the boat had been running normally.

I had six clients scheduled. These guys were well known to me, repeat clients who had been out with me at least a dozen times over the years. I was looking forward to the day, since we all knew each other well, the day would be more like a bunch of buddies getting together for the day than a charter trip. These guys were all regular, hard working, everyday type guys. They usually had a beer or two too many before the day was over, but they were a group I really did enjoy taking fishing.

We left the docks happy, and convinced the day would be a blockbuster day. On the way out this bunch always

ALASKAN DEEP SEA FISH TALES

sampled what alcoholic beverages they had brought along. To emphasize they were on a vacation trip not at work. They had never overindulged on any trip they had been out on, so I wasn't concerned when they broke out the booze bottles as we cleared the mouth of the Seldovia Bay. Conversation was active, light hearted, and varied over a number of topics.

About half way to the selected site for that days fishing, one engine broke a torque plate. This is the transfer plate that moves the power produced by the engine to the transmission. It was not a serious failure and would only take a short time to replace at the dock. I had a spare one on the boat. We decided to continue on one engine, since the water was flat the day warm and sunny, and we were half way there already. The other engine was performing flawlessly. We reasoned, if we did have engine trouble, there were tools and ample mechanical knowledge on board to replace the broken plate at sea on such a nice day.

We slowly cruised on towards the fishing hole, only making about ten knots speed. A little frustrating but not a problem. Soon the clients had imbibed a few more toddy's to help pass the time, and I noticed that one by one they were drifting off to sleep. Well, they had been up most of the night getting to Seldovia from Anchorage, and they had hit the bottle pretty hard. They would be ready to fish soon enough.

ALASKAN DEEP SEA FISH TALES

I was enjoying the fantastic weather and water conditions. The cabin doors were propped open and the smell of the ocean was fresh and clean in the air. We were now nearing my selected area for fishing and I started paying more attention to my loran coordinates, wanting to bring the boat in at the right spot to set the drift up correctly. I was slightly puzzled and aware something wasn't right, because I couldn't figure out which way I should go to finalize the drift set up. The numbers were not making sense to me. After pondering this for a little while, I stopped the boat in preparation for baiting and set up of the fishing gear.

I exited the cabin to the rear deck and pounded on the door as I left. "Time to fish, guys, wake up." One or two of them groggily sat up, bleary eyed and sluggish, not at all the normal reaction this bunch had. The guys up forward in the bunk didn't even stir. I hollered into the cabin once more, that I was baiting up, and it was time to be on deck. Finally there was motion below and I turned to the prep work on deck. I was feeling woozy and disoriented myself, and I hadn't had a thing to drink, and I hadn't been up all night either.

The slow rocking of the boat was definitely making me feel seasick. I never ever get seasick, but I was becoming more nauseous by the second. I laughingly told the guys still in the cabin, they were going to have a treat. I was going to get seasick. Disbelief was voiced back from the cabin, and a couple of them unsteadily came out on deck. I continued to bait gear until I felt suddenly, very weak and real sick. I

ALASKAN DEEP SEA FISH TALES

remember turning towards the back of the boat to puke over in the water.

The next thing I can remember is being in the water and absolutely baffled as to how I got there. Here I am about ten feet away from the boat, face down in this beautiful emerald green water, being screamed at from the rear of the boat. Ignoring the pleas from my clients, I remember just laying there thinking about how really pretty the colors were, with the shafts of sunlight shining down through the water. Something in my brain dimly told me I was contentedly laying there and drowning, and I had better do something about it. Another part of my brain was telling me it was okay and not to bother. Finally I was roused from my reverie enough by their frantic screams, that I made a half-hearted attempt to swim back to the boat. I was barely semi-conscious and not thinking coherently at all. I wasn't cold in the forty five degree water. I wasn't uncomfortable at all. If those idiots in the boat would just stop yelling, everything would be just fine. I reached the back of the boat and just lay there in the water. They couldn't reach down far enough to get me, and finally got the boat hook out, an aluminum rod with a plastic finger on the end.

As they were trying to grapple me in with the hook, I managed get shoved under the stern of the boat head first. I'm definitely drowning now. I can feel my lungs are full of water, and I still don't care. I am conscious in a detached sort of way, but really detached. They eventually

ALASKAN DEEP SEA FISH TALES

got me out from under the boat and lifted into the boat, then started trying to get the water out of my lungs. At this point I got very violently sick and pushed most of the water out along with everything else I'd eaten for a week. After this I made a phenomenal recovery. In minutes I was assuring one and all, it was time to go fishing. Walking around in sopping wet clothes, telling everyone I was fine.

This was not being accepted by anyone else but me, and they insisted we get to town ASAP so we could find out what had happened. They thought I had experienced a stroke or heart attack and were truly scared to death. With real reluctance I finally agreed to head in and went to start the boat. It took me many tries to figure out the simple procedure of starting the engines and get the boat headed into the Bay, but finally it was running and we started in.

All during the trip back we tried to figure what had happened and couldn't, we all were vaguely aware of something being really wrong, but not alarmingly so.

The wind had started blowing about ten knots out of the West on the trip back. This wind probably saved all of our lives.

After getting back to the harbor and getting checked out by a doctor, we found out I had been overcome by carbon monoxide. In fact, all of us had been affected by it. Another few minutes of running time out would have most likely caused all of our deaths. Running on one engine at

reduced speed with only a breath of wind, had allowed a build up in the cabin of the deadly gas. The only thing that prevented it from happening on the way in was the wind picking up. The next equipment installed on the boat was an active carbon monoxide sensor.
My doctor told me later, if I had not fallen into the water I probably wouldn't have survived the encounter. When people pass out from carbon monoxide, they seldom recover without medical intervention. He felt that my body had unconsciously reacted to the shock of the cold water by flooding my system with adrenaline, causing me to regain enough awareness to survive. This feeling was reinforced by my description of well being after reviving, and not being cold afterwards.

All the things that happened that day were little things. The torque plate breaking, the decision to continue, the calm air and sea, falling overboard instead of on the deck, having an experienced group aboard that reacted correctly, the guys drinking and falling asleep lowered their oxygen consumption, reaching the fishing hole before everyone was truly unconscious. They all added up to a near catastrophe, but at the same time they all added up to prevention of one.

We all go through each day thinking we are in control of our lives. This incident has made me think, we only imagine we control what happens.

ALASKAN DEEP SEA FISH TALES

THE JAPANESE/WASTE NOT

Charter operators in Alaska book clients from all over the world each season. A large portion of this tourism flow comes from Asian countries. From all of the Asian area, it is Japan that produces some of the more fervent fishing aficionados. The Japanese clients are generally very easy to satisfy, but they do expect to take home fish when they go out. Mostly they are less particular about size, and more particular about quality.

This trip had been booked for several months in advance, with numerous telephone calls confirming and re-confirming details. The clients were a group of Japanese business managers, four men, who were making their first fishing trip to Alaska. Only one of the four spoke any English language, and was barely able to communicate basic questions and needs.

When they arrived at the boat for the trip, we had a very long and complicated translation period to go through all of the safety drill, but it was all done with lots of hand signals and much smiling and laughing about the difficulty with language. The fishing gear they understood immediately. We were using electric reels manufactured in Japan. All of the instructions on the reels were printed in Japanese.

77

ALASKAN DEEP SEA FISH TALES

During the departure and on the way out to fish, they were insistent about catching fish. The one client who was acting as interpreter, repeatedly sought reassurance, they would catch some fish, yes? I assured him each time that I felt they would all catch fish before the day ended. Each time this brought smiles and head nods. A few minutes later the question would be repeated.

The day was a reasonable day, somewhat choppy seas, totally overcast with rain showers on a regular basis. Not a great day weather wise, but we were all well equipped with foul weather gear. The enthusiasm was definitely there. They were all getting more excited as I counted down the miles until we were ready to fish.

Before continuing, I should explain a couple of things. When you book a Halibut charter, you target Halibut. I don't try to catch other species, just Halibut. In Alaska, you fish for the species of fish you book the trip for. Occasionally there will be an incidental fish caught but it is fairly rare. The one particular fish a Halibut guide tries to avoid is Gray Cod. To a Halibut charter skipper, Gray Cod is like catching Carp, when you want trout, or landing Bullheads when you want Catfish. Cod is good bait, but it isn't considered classy to come in to the harbor with Cod aboard.

We arrived at the fishing hole and commenced fishing. Quickly, we had Cod on the lines, all the lines. I moved

ALASKAN DEEP SEA FISH TALES

the boat several hundred yards. More Cod, only bigger. We were landing Cod that were twenty pounds apiece. Not a sign of a Halibut though. The four Japanese fishermen were getting more excited with each hookup. I was getting more depressed.

After throwing about three hundred pounds of Cod overboard, I was ready to move to a different fishing spot, and told the clients to get ready for a move. This brought on a vigorous heated discussion, in Japanese, for several minutes. When the discussion was over, the interpreter haltingly communicated to me, his fishing partners felt I was throwing back perfectly acceptable fish that would be excellent eating. They wanted to keep the Cod. Worse, they wanted to know if there was a limit on them. There wasn't!

They were correct in saying that the fish were perfectly edible, they are, but there is a tremendous amount of waste to meat ratio and they are really nasty to clean. They smell bad when you are butchering them and they are full of bones to work around.

I told them that we were trying to catch Halibut not Cod and with a little patience, we would get the Halibut. They were not buying it. They could only catch two Halibut each. They could catch all of the Cod they wanted. They weren't seeing any Halibut. We were landing lots of Cod. Moving was democratically vetoed, by majority rule.

ALASKAN DEEP SEA FISH TALES

The boat deck was soon virtually covered with Cod, and still they came over the side. The fishermen were in hog heaven. I was trying to figure out how I was going to sneak into the harbor and get away from the boat before anyone I knew, saw my fish load. After the fish storage boxes were full and the deck completely covered with fish, they decided they had enough and gave me the, lets go home signal.

We got back to the harbor and moored the boat. Drawing the normal scattered onlookers, who quickly went elsewhere when they saw the deck. It was obvious, this guide didn't know squat about Halibut fishing.

I was preparing my knives to start cutting up the horrendous pile of Cod we had, dreading the nasty job ahead, when the interpreter explained, they wanted to butcher the fish. They would do it a certain way, and they didn't want to waste any of the delicious meat or delicacies. This definitely was agreeable with me. I was curious about what he meant about 'delicacies' though. I had never heard mere Cod mentioned this way before this.

They all formed a production line and were soon immersed in the work. I watched closely, while I did my chores on the boat. After watching for a while, I stopped. They were not only taking the meat of the fish, they were taking the stomach, the liver, the tongue, and the eyeballs. Maybe even some other parts I couldn't identify.

ALASKAN DEEP SEA FISH TALES

The one client who could speak some English, saw my distaste, and assured me that all of this was very good to eat. He then tried to explain how each part would be cooked and used. I lost even more interest at this point. He continued his work and in a surprisingly short time, they were done. They were all glowing with pride. They had accomplished what they came to Alaska for.

They all left Seldovia that afternoon with a large supply of Cod and parts. All of it carefully separated and packaged. They were very effusive in their compliments to me about the successful trip and left a substantial tip. I felt that the proverbial silk purse had just been manufactured, out of Codfish.

ALASKAN DEEP SEA FISH TALES

ALASKAN DEEP SEA FISH TALES

MIDWESTERN SIZE ADJUSTMENT

We get quite a few people who have wanted to come to Alaska for years, and for one reason or another, haven't done it until now. These kinds of bookings are always enjoyable because the clients are so overwhelmed by the scenic beauty of the country and they are boiling over with enthusiasm to catch that 'fish of a lifetime'.

This trip consisted of two middle aged couples from the Midwest. They had been friends for some number of years and were traveling together on their Alaskan fantasy vacation. Neither of these couples had ever been out on the ocean. They told me that a body of water over ten acres was a lot of water to them. I was somewhat apprehensive about their reaction to the big water of the ocean but it was a nice day. They were confident they would be able to handle the ocean without seasickness, and they were all bursting with eagerness to get on with the day.

It was a routine kind of day. Nice everything. The clients were friendly and happy. They asked all of the usual first timer questions as we were running, and were genuinely interested in the behind the scenes operation of a charter business.

ALASKAN DEEP SEA FISH TALES

We soon reached the spot for that day. Shortly after that everyone was fishing intensely. All talking excitedly about the scenery and the massive emptiness of the ocean. They were all very comfortable with everything and none of them showed even a hint of the dreaded seasickness.

This particular day had a fairly large tidal flow, something in the range of twenty feet. I had told them earlier the fishing would be spotty as long as the tide was running hard but it would get better during the slowdown and turnaround. We had started fishing in the middle of the tide flow, so I wasn't too surprised when the bites were slow to start. I reiterated what I had said earlier about the tide and urged them to enjoy the nice day. We had a lot of fishing time in front of us to enjoy.

After about thirty or forty minutes of next to no action, we finally started getting light hits. Halibut we call 'chickens' were finding the bait and chewing on it. These fish are immature Halibut under fifteen pounds. There were numerous hits and hookups, but nothing stayed on the hook long enough to boat it. I again assured them it would happen, just have patience.

The initial enthusiasm had slowed down a little and three of the clients were inside the cabin getting a snack and warming up. I was telling my usual guide stories and not really concerned. I was positive we would do fine before the day ended.

ALASKAN DEEP SEA FISH TALES

My fourth person, one of the men, had continued to fish and finally hooked a small 'chicken' solidly enough to land it. I was waiting beside him as the fish surfaced. I lifted the fish aboard carefully and released the hook from its jaw. The fisherman was going nuts, he was hollering at the others and his wife. This was excitement for him. While all of the commotion was going on I picked up the small fish about ten pounds, held it up for them to see in the cabin, and dropped it back into the water. When the fish dropped into the water the smiles disappeared.

The man who had landed the fish turned to me with a look on his face that was not happy. He started having a total fit at me for throwing his fish back. The biggest fish he had caught in his entire life, and I threw it back without even asking or letting them take a picture. For a time, I seriously thought I was going to get punched. The others were trying to make light of it, but I could sense a feeling of displeasure. We had been fishing for a hour and didn't have any fish in the boat, and the dumb skipper throws back the biggest fish any of them had ever caught.

I tried to explain my motives and soothe the fisherman's feelings. Telling him that we just didn't keep fish that small only added fuel to the fire. Soon there was only grumpy silence on the fishing deck. Punctuated occasionally by comments about the idiot skipper they had hired. As the minutes added up and then the hours started adding up, the comments became more frequent and more to the point.

ALASKAN DEEP SEA FISH TALES

About four more hours went by and we didn't land another fish. The tension had reached a high stress level. I knew the fish were down there, we just couldn't get them to take the bait solidly enough to hook them. Doggedly, I kept repeating the mantra, it will be okay, they will come.

The abuse from the unhappy fisherman was now reaching a point of outright insults. In four hours he had not calmed down at all, in reality he had become madder. Continuing to tell them the fish would eventually bite wasn't helping things either. They could plainly see the fish weren't biting.

By now I was beginning to doubt my own beliefs and was seriously considering calling the trip a 'freebie' to try and assuage the clients. We were right at the tidal slack and the fish still hadn't started hitting. I felt really bad.

Then, almost miraculously, Halibut started hitting. We went from no bites to two and three nice fish on at once. The upset fisherman landed a seventy pounder and I was suddenly the greatest guide in Alaska. Every one of the clients landed their limit in about thirty minutes. The smallest fish of the day was forty five pounds and the largest was ninety eight. Everyone was extremely nice and apologetic for the hours of griping.

I told them I had understood their apprehension, but doing the trips every day, I did know what was happening out on the fishing grounds. If I had kept the little fish, they would

ALASKAN DEEP SEA FISH TALES

have been disappointed later on. They pointed out that the fish was not a 'little' fish where they came from. I explained that I understood that part too.

The day ended well with no hard feelings. As they left that day they assured me their fish size attitude would be adjusted for future trips. These two couples have fished with me several times since that day and sure enough, they now know what a small fish means in Alaska.

If these clients ever read this story, they'll know how nervous and worried I was that afternoon. If those fish hadn't started biting I'd have been a real dummy in their eyes. I have had days too, when I was wrong, and we didn't catch anything. Luckily this time wasn't one of those. I gained some good clients and friends who now believe Alaska is a special place to visit.

ALASKAN DEEP SEA FISH TALES

ALASKAN DEEP SEA FISH TALES

OUR PROBLEM=THEIR RESCUE

We were fishing about twenty five miles out in the Central Inlet. It was blowing and rough. Seas were averaging six feet with very close spacing. This was making for a very rough ride whether we were fishing or moving, there was lots of motion. I had four experienced fishermen aboard, all doctors, who were determined to catch their limit before quitting. The sun was shining and despite the rough seas, we were all enjoying the day. Substantial sized fish were being caught and there was enough steady action to keep everyone occupied.

We were returning to the start of a drift, when I ran over a large piece of discarded cargo netting. Unseen in the rough water, the heavy netting jammed in the turning propellers stalling the engines before I even realized what was happening.

When the engines stalled the boat immediately turned sideways to the waves and began rocking strongly. There was no danger in this, but it sure made movement on the boat difficult. We soon understood what had happened. We could see part of the coarse, kelp covered net, sticking out by the stern.

ALASKAN DEEP SEA FISH TALES

After getting the transmissions in neutral and restarting the engines I kept shifting in and out of gear trying to free up at least one propeller. After numerous attempts and a lot of cutting away pieces of net, we managed to get the port side prop cleared. We could at least maneuver the boat now. Every trick we tried on the starboard side failed. There was just too much webbing jammed in the prop and rudder to be able to free it. If the water had been calm it might have been possible to go into the water and cut it free but in the rough seas we had, it wasn't even thinkable.

We decided to drift free for a short while, trying to catch the last few fish we needed. This was successful and we started what we all knew to be a long run back to the harbor. On one engine the boat would only run at about six knots with the wad of net dragging in the water. It was difficult to steer also because of the drag on one side of the boat. It would take about three to four hours longer than normal to run in. Not a fun way to spend an afternoon.

The big ball of jammed net did have one positive to it. The drag in the water helped to minimize the rolling of the hull in the steep waves.

We had been under way for about two hours when there was a Mayday distress call on the radio. We listened to the unfolding drama as the Coast Guard attempted to identify the nature of the distress. The Coast Guard was having difficulty hearing the boat in trouble. We were getting blown out of our seats with a strong signal.

ALASKAN DEEP SEA FISH TALES

As the situation unfolded it was clear their were some people in serious trouble somewhere on the ocean waters nearby. There were four men aboard a twenty one foot boat. The boat had been swamped with a large wave, the engines were under water and the boat was sinking. They had no firm idea of their position, only an approximation and there was not any navigational radio equipment aboard.

The ocean is a very large place. When you are several miles offshore it is easy to misidentify your position by a large margin. In rough seas with a small sinking boat as a target, the task of finding this small target gets immeasurably large. We listened as the panic grew in the distressed fisherman's voice pleading for help, as the boat helplessly sank out from under them. The last plea from the boat was to please hurry assistance, the radio was going under water.

The Coast Guard only received a garbled part of this message, we heard it loud and clear. I radioed to the Coast Guard our position and circumstances. When I told them we were clearly receiving the radio signals from the sinking boat, they requested we search the area near our course as well as we could. We had already started to actively look for any signs of the other boat. The Coast Guard was dispatching a cutter from Homer, nearly thirty miles from the site.

ALASKAN DEEP SEA FISH TALES

For about thirty minutes we looked and circled, not seeing anything. It was difficult with the waves and wind to identify anything although we had spotted several large pieces of driftwood. I was in steady contact with the Search and Rescue people by radio. The steadily increasing helpless feeling was one of disaster. After this length of time in the icy waters, there was little chance of survivors. Fifteen to thirty minutes is the useful expected time of survival in Alaskan ocean water.

We had just completed a run and turned the boat to the East, the sun was behind us and I wanted to use that back lighting to see towards the distant land more clearly. I started another run going Southeasterly and was nervously hoping to see something in the water anything at all out of the ordinary.

While I was driving the boat, my clients were also scanning the water in all directions. Suddenly one of them said that he thought he saw something off of our stern, almost directly into the bright sun. I was skeptical but turned the boat in the direction he was pointing. We ran for several minutes without seeing anything in the tossing seas, still six to seven feet high. Again my client said he saw something, ahead and to the right. I looked in the direction indicated and saw a mass of driftwood. Telling him it was only a log, I started to turn back towards shore. As the boat was turning one of the others said that he saw something off in the distance. We started plowing through the water in that direction.

ALASKAN DEEP SEA FISH TALES

Very soon we could see that this was the boat we were looking for. There were four people clinging to the bow railing that was sticking up out of the water about three feet. All were frantically waving as we approached. It seemed to take forever to reach them at the speed we were able to maintain. I radioed the Rescue Center telling them we had found them and gave the coordinates to the still distant cutter.

Reaching the boat we saw that it had completely sunk, trapping a pocket of water in the bow section. It was floating straight up with the nose in the air. This had allowed the men to keep a portion of their bodies out of the cold water. The men were completely panicked when we got there and we had a few minor difficulties getting them into my boat, both from the rough seas, but complicated by their worsening fear and hypothermic conditions. After several scares and unsuccessful attempts we had all four on board.

Amidst a chaotic scene of bedraggled, grateful, panic stricken fishermen, we all gave thanks for the problem that had caused us to be in the area at all. Without the net in the props, we would have still been miles out on the water or in the harbor.

The Coast Guard cutter arrived on the scene, dwarfing my small charter boat. They launched outboard powered inflatable boats and a crew of experienced rescue people soon had the men transferred to the cutter and long hot showers.

After the Rescue personnel had hoisted the mostly sunken boat aboard the cutter, we received warm thanks for our part in the rescue from the Captain of the cutter. We were given baseball caps with the cutter logo on them, then continued our way into Seldovia harbor.

After reaching the dock it was a relatively simple matter to remove the netting and be ready to run the next day.

I never heard from any of the four rescued men after that day. I did find out, through the Coast Guard, they were all fine by the time the cutter had reached Homer.

Another adventure awaits tomorrow. If not then, sometime in the near future.

… ALASKAN DEEP SEA FISH TALES

THE TOW

Nearly every year my charter boat is called upon to tow a disabled boat in to safe harbor. It is a daily occurrence for someone to break down somewhere in the Kachemak Bay or lower Cook Inlet. There is a large charter fleet operating in these waters and a huge fleet of personal boats. On top of this there are several hundred commercial boats operating seasonally in the same areas.

These numbers would lead the first time observer to think it wouldn't be hard to get help in an emergency. This would be an incorrect observation. The waters of this area are vast beyond description. There are many times when you know there are several hundred boats active, and you can see no other activity in any direction as far as you can see. This is nice if you want privacy and solitude while you fish. Its not so nice if there is a true emergency.

I had six fishermen on board and we were on our way in from a successful day of fishing. The weather was clear and the water calm. We were enjoying the ride and the scenery. The big diesels in the boat were singing their smooth turbo charged songs, the fish boxes were full of fish, all was well in the world.

ALASKAN DEEP SEA FISH TALES

We were still several miles off shore when I noticed a small speck off in the distance in front of us. I was slightly off of our course and I assumed it was another boat fishing for Halibut. We had almost reached a point abeam of this boat, still nearly a mile away, when one of the clients said he had seen a red flare.

Pulling the throttles back on my boat, I turned the wheel to head us towards the boat. Soon two other flares were sighted. There was one man on the disabled boat shooting flares off and waving a cloth object in the air.

We pulled up beside the boat, a twenty two foot wooden cabin cruiser, with one inboard engine and outdrive. Inquiring what the problem was, I was told he needed a tow, his engine had stopped and he couldn't restart it. I radioed the Coast Guard and informed them of the situation and told them we would shortly have the disabled boat in tow.

Before starting to hook up I asked all of the normal questions. Had he tried this or checked fuel etc.. Soon I discovered that his engine was flooded, but with water. The reason he needed a tow was his boat was leaking badly and the engine was under water up to the spark plugs. He had been slightly reluctant to say the boat was sinking.

As we were readying a tow line, I questioned as to why the boat had started taking on water badly enough to threaten sinking. I found out that he had known of wood rot around

ALASKAN DEEP SEA FISH TALES

the stern of the boat but had patched it up with epoxy. He had felt that the bilge pump would take care of the small amount of water that was still leaking into the boat. Evidently the thrust and vibration of the engine had cracked the seams loose around the stern. We continued to talk back and forth about the tow and what I would do once under tow. In this short time the water had risen another three or four inches in his boat. He was highly concerned, rightfully so, about salvaging as much value from the salt water laden boat as possible. Shortly we had the tow rope attached to the bow of his boat and the stern of mine and I eased the throttles forward to start the long tow into Seldovia.

The bow of his boat came up quickly and sharply out of the water, with the stern settling lower as the motion and angles moved the water inside the boat back to the lowest point in the back. He radioed on the CB for me to increase speed if I could, as his engine was totally under water now. He hoped to use the speed of the boat to get it up on step and allow the water to drain out the back of the boat through the cracked areas.

I fed more power to the engines and soon we were up to about sixteen knots. The towed boat was not towing well at all. The stern was very low in the water and the bow continued to stick way up in the air. He radioed that he was going to try bailing with a cooler while we were under way and to try to increase the speed even more if possible. I told him there would be no problem with more speed, but

ALASKAN DEEP SEA FISH TALES

I was concerned about the erratic way the boat was responding. He insisted that more speed would help get rid of the water.

My boat has twin three hundred and fifteen horsepower Yanmar turbo charged diesels in it, running through full hydraulic transmissions with reduction gears. It can cruise at thirty knots and run flat out at thirty five. It is an extremely powerful boat and I was slightly apprehensive as I increased the power again. Hearing the big diesels start to sing as the turbos spooled up, I saw on the GPS we were making over nineteen knots and accelerating.

Looking out to the back of the boat I saw the other boat suddenly swerve sharply. Before I could even reach for the throttles, the other boat completely disintegrated in a burst of pieces. My clients and I were all in a state of disbelief as I quickly turned my boat back towards the mass of debris that had just recently been a semi-functional boat.

We found the owner of the boat immediately and recovered him from the water. He was in a mild state of shock himself as he explained what had happened.

When we had started the tow, the water had surged to the back of his boat, putting a lot of pressure on the weakened stern. He had tried to bail it with the cooler but water was still coming in faster than it was going out. The last speed increase had lowered the stern even more.

ALASKAN DEEP SEA FISH TALES

He told us in a tone of disbelief that the entire stern, engine and outdrive has simply snapped out of the boat with no warning. This mass of weight disappearing is what caused the sharp swerve. With the entire stern gone, the sides of the boat just collapsed and the boat fell apart.

He wanted, understandably, to salvage anything of value from the wreckage and after informing the Coast Guard about what had happened we started picking through the floating debris.

I maneuvered my boat close to a large piece of the cabin and tried to get a grip on it with the boat hook. Hooking the plastic hook through a window edge, I applied pressure to bring the piece closer. The whole window frame broke away in crumbling chunks. I tried again on a section of hull and pushed the plastic hook completely through the side of the floating hull. I commented to the owner that I was really unimpressed with the condition of the used-to-be boat.

He was searching through the floating pieces with my long handled gaff and miraculously recovered his personal bag. It had all of his money and ID in it, along with a three fifty seven magnum pistol. He was quite glad to have recovered this. I wondered quietly if he might use the pistol on me or my clients in distress over the loss of his boat. But that was only a fleeting thought. He was happy to have been found before the boat sank. He knew the boat was in poor condition, but had taken it out to fish because it was a nice day and he thought he might get another season or two out of the old boat. Moral of this story is, don't ever go to sea in a leaky boat.

ALASKAN DEEP SEA FISH TALES

THE VOYAGE

The boat that I am currently using for charter work, a thirty four foot Bayliner with a thirteen foot beam, was purchased from a party in Valdez, Alaska. Valdez is located at the head of Prince William Sound approximately two hundred and seventy miles by water from Seldovia, our home port. My daughter, now in her twenties, had arranged all of the details of the purchase. I completely trusted her knowledge and judgment on the purchase because she had worked with me for several years during the charter season. She knew absolutely what I was going to expect out of the boat and she was enthusiastic about it. I committed to the boat purchase, sight unseen.

The only hesitation I had with the purchase concerned the engines. They were gasoline powered, and I had previously vowed never to own another gas powered boat. The engines in this boat were very low time engines and appeared to be in good condition, so I decided to go for the deal.

The final arrangements were done through my daughter while I was out of the State. We had dozens of phone calls, working out the details, but after several delays the boat was ours.

ALASKAN DEEP SEA FISH TALES

I made plans and set dates for moving the boat from Valdez to Seldovia. My wife and daughter would accompany me when I took the boat to Seldovia. We estimated we would make the trip in one long day. Daylight was available virtually continuously during June in Alaska, when we intended on doing the move.

My daughter arranged for many of the necessary minor maintenance items to be done in the Valdez boatyard, while the boat was dry-docked, then had the boat launched and in a slip before I arrived.

She met my wife and I at the Valdez airport, excited and proud of all she had done for us. We were informed that the boat was ready for final tests by me and all we would need to do was provision it for the run to Seldovia.

Shortly we were at the Valdez boat harbor and aboard the new boat. I was immensely pleased with the boat itself, but I saw many things that pointed to owner neglect. The wood trim was in poor condition and the bilges of the boat were filthy. Not wanting to deflate my daughter's accomplishments I kept relatively quiet about these minor concerns. A little elbow grease would fix these problems.

The boat was beautiful in its layout and lines. A classic white, sleek Sportfisherman hull and flying bridge made her look larger than she was, and the wide beam looked awesome. It performed very nicely out on the Bay, but

ALASKAN DEEP SEA FISH TALES

testing showed that the speed quoted by the former owner was not there and fuel consumption was higher than anticipated. Other boat purchasers have experienced these things too, I'm sure.

I ran over and over the computations on fuel and speed vs. the distance to our destination. Three hundred and thirty gallons of gasoline filled the tanks. I figured to have a reserve we would need to have at least another two hundred gallons on board. We arranged to place four fifty five gallon drums of fuel on the back deck along with full tanks.

The morning of our departure dawned picture perfect as we had hoped it would be. The forecast was for seas of three feet or less. We were excited and anxious to be on our way. After my wife had prepared a great breakfast in the galley, the three of us left the Valdez harbor at six thirty A.M. with all systems functional and five hundred and forty gallons of gasoline aboard. I felt as if I was driving a floating bomb as we started our run down the Bay towards Prince William Sound.

We had completely perfect running conditions as we entered the Sound. Before long we had passed Bligh Reef made famous by that errant oil tanker skipper. The water was calm and we saw a lot of sea life.

About fifty miles into our trip I decided to top off the tanks from the drums to double check our usage and to get the

combustible liquid off the deck as soon as I could. Using a diaphragm pump, my daughter and I transferred fuel while my wife drove. We emptied one drum then started on a second. It disappeared into the tank and we still hadn't topped off. The third drum was set up and we pumped some more. About ten gallons into it we topped off the tank. I sat down at the helm and started doing mental arithmetic. It didn't take much to figure out that my fuel usage and mileage figures were way off.
No problem, we would alter our route slightly and refuel in Seward, stay overnight and continue the trip the next day. It would be a little more expensive than calculated but not anything other than an inconvenience. The boat was running well and the seas calm, warm sunshine made driving from the flying bridge a pleasure, the views of Prince William Sound were unsurpassable.

Hours later we entered Resurrection Bay. Seward is situated at the very top of the bay, twelve miles in from the open sea. About two miles into the bay, the right engine of the boat started backfiring and varying its RPM. The water temp of the engine started climbing too. Stopping, we checked it out and found the coolant level very low. It had been full when we left Valdez. After topping the coolant and checking out the distributor the engine seemed to settle down and we continued into the Seward harbor with no trouble. I docked the boat at the fuel dock and topped off everything we had. Valdez to Seward, about half of our trip, had consumed three hundred and twenty seven gallons of gasoline. We were burning almost fifty percent more

ALASKAN DEEP SEA FISH TALES

than I calculated. Good thing we had been cautious. There aren't any fuel sources between Seward and Seldovia. We obtained temporary moorage, had a fine meal on shore at one of the waterfront restaurants and were back on board ready for a good nights rest, by eight P.M..

After getting back aboard, I got nervous about the engine acting up and decided to really check it out while in the harbor. We had plenty of tools and spare ignition parts, so I crawled into the engine room and started my inspection. I found only minor problems, replaced the points and one set of plug wires. We tested the engine and it sounded fine. I was slightly apprehensive about the coolant disappearance but not overly so. I went to sleep confident that the rest of the trip would be a non-event.

Next morning we were up at six and raring to go. Clearing the harbor before seven, it appeared we would have another beautiful day in which to complete our trip. The boat was running strong and felt as if it was running much smoother than the previous day.

About twelve miles out of Seward, the right engine high temp alarm went off. Opening the engine room, I found steam and coolant everywhere. We had blown a head gasket. There was nothing to do but return to Seward on one engine. As my wife and daughter drove the boat slowly back, I started disassembling the engine to make repairs.

ALASKAN DEEP SEA FISH TALES

By the time we arrived back at the harbor I had most of the engine apart and had determined the head gasket had failed between two cylinders and the outside of the engine block. My wife got acquainted with the local parts suppliers while my daughter and I turned wrenches. The rest of that day and most of the night was spent doing the necessary repairs.

The next morning we departed again, this time into dense fog. Fog was not a navigational problem as the boat was completely equipped with electronic equipment and radar. Navigating in the fog does take a lot more attention though and my wife doesn't like it at all. About twenty five miles out of Seward we ran out of the fog into low overcast gray skies. Gusty wind was starting and there were small whitecaps. The weather forecast still indicated seas of three feet or less. Another forty miles went by uneventfully.

The new head gasket failed shortly thereafter. We spent some time trying to understand why the new gasket had failed, but without taking the engine apart again there was no way to know. It was leaking coolant steadily out the front corner of the engine block. The engine was running okay, but obviously there was no guarantee it would continue to do so. We were almost exactly half way between Seward and Seldovia so I elected to continue at a reduced speed to baby the sick engine along. Also raising our fuel consumption. It eventually turned out to be a warped head causing all the trouble.

ALASKAN DEEP SEA FISH TALES

We ran like this for several hours. I drove the boat, my daughter kept feeding the sick engine more coolant, and my wife worried. The weather was getting nastier all the time. As we neared the tip of the Kenai Peninsula, our final turning point to Seldovia twenty five miles away, the seas were running about eight feet. We were running about as fast as we would have been able to if the engines had been healthy. The boat was riding the seas nicely and in between checking the coolant level on the bad engine, my daughter was on the flying bridge with me. We were having a ball watching the seas breaking over the bow and enjoying the feel of the twenty thousand pound boat smoothly pushing its way through the walls of green water. There was a lot of motion, but it was not jarring. My wife had secluded herself in the mid stateroom bunk, convinced that my daughter and I were both insane. She saw nothing invigorating about the seas or the motion of the boat through them.

When we turned the corner at the tip of the Peninsula we could see sun shining on the water several miles ahead. The waves had started to subside as soon as we rounded the tip of land.

Soon we were running in sunshine and much calmer water. The rest of the trip into Seldovia was uneventful with the exception of the magnificent views we were seeing in the clearing weather.

ALASKAN DEEP SEA FISH TALES

We arrived in Seldovia fifteen hours after leaving Seward, about double the expected time. Total fuel consumption for the trip from Valdez was six hundred and fifty four gallons. A lot more than calculated. I decided right then and there to repower the just purchased boat with diesels. A decision I have not regretted for a moment. With the diesels we increased the boats cruising speed by nearly ten knots and at the same time cut our fuel usage by fifty percent.

At the time this is written we are still using this boat in our operation and I feel my daughter picked out a great boat.

ALASKAN DEEP SEA FISH TALES

AN AIRPLANE STORY

No book about Alaska fishing would be complete without at least one story about an airplane, since it is nearly impossible to do any serious fishing in Alaska without encountering the use of small aircraft.

In the early days of my charter operation, I flew clients out of Anchorage each day to Seldovia, fished all day then returned them to Anchorage each evening. It made for extremely long arduous days but was generally quite rewarding. I owned a Cessna 206, a six passenger three hundred horsepower single engine airplane. Usually I had four clients each day. Eventually I had to discontinue this service because of operational costs and new regulations.

On this particular trip, the fishing had gone well and my clients were happy to be in the air and on the way back to Anchorage. I had a fully loaded airplane and four tired clients aboard. We departed Seldovia about two hours earlier than usual due to excellent fishing and weather, and I was particularly looking forward to a full nights sleep instead of the usual four or five hours that was normal during the busy season.

About twenty or twenty five minutes into the flight all of the fishermen were asleep or about to be sleeping. I was enjoying the clear smooth air and the spectacular Alaskan scenery on the one hundred and forty mile flight to

ALASKAN DEEP SEA FISH TALES

Anchorage. Everything was functioning one hundred percent normally as we flew over Tustemena Lake on the Kenai Peninsula.

I had just finished a casual scan of the engine instruments, all were normal, when the engine went instantaneously from a smooth powerful drone to a crashing, vibrating, shaking mess. It was shaking so badly that I had trouble reading the instruments, which were still reading normal. Obviously they had not received the message about what was going on, because I knew without consulting them, that the engine was no longer operating normally.

About now numerous things were happening inside the airplane. I decided I would rather be anywhere else, and the suddenly wide awake clients decided we were about to crash. There was a large amount of black oil spraying on the windows and windshield on the pilots side of the plane reinforcing my feeling of a catastrophic problem. Simultaneously I tried to assess the trouble and assure my clients that we were not in immediate danger of crashing, although it was a possibility in the not too distant future.

The engine continued to run although very weakly and with severe vibration. I could not keep the plane from slowly losing altitude even with a wide open throttle. Whatever had happened was severely limiting the output of power from the engine and indications were that it would quit altogether any second.

ALASKAN DEEP SEA FISH TALES

Calling Kenai airport tower on the radio I declared an emergency, telling them I was trying to reach Soldotna airport before we ran out of altitude or the engine stopped.

I carefully explained the situation to my clients, and encouraged them to help me scan for satisfactory emergency landing spots. We slowly progressed toward Soldotna losing altitude steadily. I had finally stabilized the airplane at about one hundred and ten miles an hour and three hundred feet per minute loss of air under us. The oil continued to pour out across the windshield and the engine continued its erratic shaking and shuddering. I was most concerned that if the engine quit suddenly at low altitude we wouldn't have time to find a place to safely land without wrecking the plane. I kept thinking that this couldn't really be happening to me. I took meticulous care of my plane and the engine only had eight hundred hours on it. None of these thoughts changed anything, it was happening, and it wasn't going to be pretty if I couldn't nurse the sick airplane to the runway at Soldotna.

After what seemed to be forever but was only a few minutes, I could see the runway at Soldotna, several miles ahead of us. Calculating the air left under us and the distance to the runway, I felt it was going to be extremely close whether we made the airport or not. I added the last bit of throttle to the engine and literally prayed that it wouldn't quit in the next few minutes. As bad as it was shaking I couldn't understand how it was still running at

ALASKAN DEEP SEA FISH TALES

all. My four fishermen were absolutely silent during the continuing crisis.

After what seemed to me an eternity, we were lined up with the end of the long wide runway. As we cleared the perimeter fence at the airport I noted that we had less than three hundred feet of altitude. One more minute of flying time further away and I would have had to crash land the plane.

Landing the plane as quickly as possible, I turned off of the runway at the first taxiway intersection and shut the engine down. Everyone was cheering and congratulating me on the safe landing as we exited the plane. All were happy to be safely on the ground, myself included.

A short time later, I began removing the cowling from the engine compartment to find out what damage had occurred. Removing the top cowl showed me that we had experienced a minor miracle. The center cylinder on the left side of the six cylinder pancake style engine was completely destroyed. I do mean completely destroyed. There was a huge ragged hole in the side of the engine where the cylinder should have been. Pieces of engine and shrapnel were all over the engine compartment. A fuel injector line was sheared off. The connecting rod had broken at the crankshaft boss sometime during the first seconds of failure, allowing the engine to keep turning. How all of the destruction had happened without locking the engine up I will never know. There turned out to be

ALASKAN DEEP SEA FISH TALES

less than a quart of oil left in the engine crankcase. It was clear that the plane wasn't going to fly any more that day. I informed the Kenai controllers by radio that we had made the airfield safely, and we secured the airplane in an unused tiedown spot.

We ended up having to rent a vehicle and drive back to Anchorage from Soldotna. This seemed to be agreeable to all, considering the other options that could have taken place. All of the fish caught that day was salvaged without spoilage, and the clients agreed they had experienced a unique fishing experience. I was down for nearly a week as the aircraft repair crew had to replace the entire engine. That season was not a profitable one. The new engine and related expenses, lost trips etc. came to nearly twenty thousand dollars.

In all my years of flying in Alaska, this was the only actual in-flight emergency I ever experienced in many thousands of hours of flight time. If I never have another experience of this kind it will be fine with me.

ALASKAN DEEP SEA FISH TALES

ALASKAN DEEP SEA FISH TALES